Create Your Own Website

Third Edition

SCOTT MITCHELL

SAMS 800 East 96th Street, Indianapolis, Indiana 46240

Create Your Own Website

Copyright © 2007 by Pearson Education, Inc.

International Standard Book Number: 0-672-32926-3

Printed in the United States of America

First Printing: September 2006

09   08   07   06   5   4   3   2

Trademarks

All terms mentioned in this book that are known to be trademarks or service marks have been appropriately capitalized. Sams Publishing cannot attest to the accuracy of this information. Use of a term in this book should not be regarded as affecting the validity of any trademark or service mark.

Warning and Disclaimer

Every effort has been made to make this book as complete and as accurate as possible, but no warranty or fitness is implied. The information provided is on an "as is" basis. The author and the publisher shall have neither liability nor responsibility to any person or entity with respect to any loss or damages arising from the information contained in this book or from the use of the CD or programs accompanying it.

Bulk Sales

Sams Publishing offers excellent discounts on this book when ordered in quantity for bulk purchases or special sales. For more information, please contact

> **U.S. Corporate and Government Sales**
> **1-800-382-3419**
> **corpsales@pearsontechgroup.com**

For sales outside of the U.S., please contact

> **International Sales**
> **international@pearsoned.com**

Library of Congress Cataloging-in-Publication Data

Mitchell, Scott.
   Create your own website / Scott Mitchell. -- 3rd ed.
      p. cm.
   ISBN 0-672-32926-3 (pbk. : alk. paper) 1. Web sites--Design. I. Title.
TK5105.888.M57 2006b
006.7--dc22
                              2006024170

Editor-in-Chief
Karen Gettman

Acquisitions Editor
Neil Rowe

Development Editor
Mark Renfrow

Managing Editor
Gina Kanouse

Project Editor
Christy Hackerd

Copy Editor
Jennifer Cramer

Indexer
Lisa Stumpf

Proofreader
Christy Hackerd

Compositor
Michael Thurston

Technical Editor
Doug Holland

Publishing Coordinator
Cindy Teeters

Multimedia Developer
Dan Scherf

Book Designer
Gary Adair

Contents at a Glance

Table of Contents

About the Author

Create Your Own Website is author **Scott Mitchell**'s seventh book, his others being: *Sams Teach Yourself Active Server Pages 3.0 in 21 Days* (Sams); *Designing Active Server Pages* (O'Reilly); *ASP.NET: Tips, Tutorials, and Code* (Sams); *ASP.NET Data Web Controls Kick Start* (Sams); *Teach Yourself ASP.NET in 24 Hours* (Sams); and *Teach Youself ASP.NET 2.0 in 24 Hours* (Sams). Scott has also written dozens of magazine articles, as well as over one thousand online articles on his website, 4GuysFromRolla.com.

Scott's non-writing accomplishments include speaking at numerous technical user groups and conferences across the country. Scott has also taught numerous web technology classes at the University of California—San Diego University Extension. In addition to teaching and writing, Scott also is a software developer. He works as an independent consultant and has authored and sold a number of commercial software applications.

Scott lives in San Diego, California with his wife, Jisun, and dog, Sam. You can learn more about Scott at http://www.4GuysFromRolla.com/ScottMitchell or at his blog, http://www.ScottOnWriting.net.

Dedication

Can I get a shout out for the septuagenarians of the world?

Acknowledgments

Special thanks to the professional and knowledgeable folks at Sams Publishing. This is my sixth book published with Sams, and it has been as rewarding and enjoyable an experience as the five previous titles.

We Want to Hear from You!

As the reader of this book, *you* are our most important critic and commentator. We value your opinion and want to know what we're doing right, what we could do better, what areas you'd like to see us publish in, and any other words of wisdom you're willing to pass our way.

As publisher for Sams Publishing, I welcome your comments. You can email or write me directly to let me know what you did or didn't like about this book—as well as what we can do to make our books better.

Please note that I cannot help you with technical problems related to the topic of this book. We do have a User Services group, however, where I will forward specific technical questions related to the book.

When you write, please be sure to include this book's title and author as well as your name, email address, and phone number. I will carefully review your comments and share them with the author and editors who worked on the book.

Email: feedback@samspublishing.com

Mail: Paul Boger
         Publisher
         Sams Publishing
         800 East 96th Street
         Indianapolis, IN 46240 USA

For more information about this book or another Sams Publishing title, visit our website at www.samspublishing.com. Type the ISBN (excluding hyphens) or the title of a book in the Search field to find the page you're looking for.

Welcome to Create Your Own Website!

As the popularity of the Internet and the World Wide Web have risen since its beginnings in the early 1990s, virtually all businesses have established an online presence. Many individuals, too, have left their imprints on the web, creating a website for their family, or posting pictures of their vacations. If you want to join the millions of people who have created websites, but fear you lack the background or expertise for such an endeavor, this book is for you!

In this book you'll see just how easy creating a website can be. The CD included with this book contains four professional website templates and a free web page editor. With the web page editor you can quickly and easily customize the provided templates into your very own personal websites. Using the web page editor is as simple as using a word processor program. It's just point and click!

Since there are a number of different types of websites on the Internet, this book's CD includes four different templates for four different types of sites. Specifically, the four provided templates will let you quickly create the following types of sites:

1. **Family websites**—With a family website you can share pictures of you and your family with friends and members of your extended family.

2. **Hobby websites**—A hobby website allows you to share your hobbies with others who have similar interests.

3. **Community websites**—With a community website your church, club, bowling team, or other group or association can post information, schedules, pictures, and other pertinent information.

4. **Online storefront website**—Sell products online by accepting credit card payments with an online storefront site.

In addition to showing you how to build your own websites from the ground up, this book also includes four chapters on how to use existing web applications to quickly create common websites. Specifically, you'll see how to:

▶ **Sell products at eBay Stores**—eBay Stores are a quick and easy way to start selling products online. With eBay Stores, your products are listed on eBay.com and payment processing is handled for you by eBay. You simply list your products for sale and ship them when purchased!

▶ **Publish content online with a blog**—A blog is a type of website designed to allow a user to quickly and easily publish content online. Blogs are springing up all over the World Wide Web, used by both individuals and businesses alike.

▶ **Share your digital pictures**—You've just gotten back from your vacation to Tahiti with gobs of digital pictures. How do you easily share these beautiful pictures with your friends and family? Digital picture sharing websites make it easy to upload your pictures, share them with select friends and family, and order prints.

▶ **Create a Homepage on MySpace**—MySpace is one of many "social networking" websites, where visitors can stay in touch with friends, meet their friends' friends, and make new social contacts. In addition to maintaining and growing your network of friends, MySpace makes it easy for you to create your own web pages, post pictures, share music, and host a blog.

Whether you want to build your own, unique website or use a pre-existing web application, you'll learn everything you need to know to start building your own website today with this book. Get ready to see just how fun and easy it is to create your very own websites!

CHAPTER 1

Creating Your First Web Page

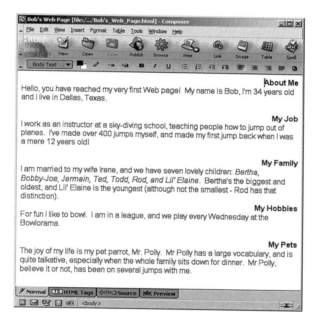

Have you ever wanted to create your own website, but thought that the task was too daunting? Do you think that only folks with years of computer training and experience have the knowledge necessary for building web pages? These are common misconceptions that many people have. With the right tools and information, creating websites is as easy as pointing and clicking! If you are interested in quickly creating a professional-looking website, then you've picked up the right book.

> **NOTE**
>
> Don't have any website building experience? Don't worry! This book's CD contains professional website templates that you can use to build your own website within minutes. You'll also learn how to use existing website applications to sell products, publish content, and share images online.

This book includes a CD with website templates, along with software for editing the web templates. In this chapter, you'll look at the fundamental building blocks of websites, and then step through the installation process of Mozilla Composer, the web page creation software included on the CD. In the next chapter you'll examine the necessary steps to create a website, and see how to move the web page templates from the CD to your website. Chapters 3 and 4 illustrate how the templates on the book's CD can be customized to create your own website.

In addition to the website templates, Chapters 5 through 7 examine online tools that assist in creating websites. Specifically, you'll learn how

to sell products through a website using eBay Stores, publish content through a blog at Blogger.com, and share images and prints with friends and family via SnapFish.com.

While there are literally millions of websites available on the Internet, virtually all fall into one of three categories:

▶ **Family/Personal Website**—Keep your extended family and friends up to date with the latest happenings of your family.

▶ **Online Storefront Website**—Sell products and services online! A great revenue stream for home-based businesses.

▶ **Content Publishing Website**—Publish your content on the World Wide Web. Be it your poetry or stories or your political or philosophical views, by distributing your content online you open it up to a potential world-wide audience of millions.

As you'll see, creating websites that fall into any of these three categories is a snap with the provided templates and website tools. To get started, all you'll need is this book, its CD, and access to a computer with Internet connectivity.

> *"Creating websites is a snap with the provided templates. To get started, all you'll need is this book, its CD, and access to a computer with Internet connectivity."*

In addition to examining how to build web pages from scratch, you'll also learn how to use existing website applications to build your own website. Chapter 5 looks at how to use eBay Stores to start selling online, while Chapter 6 examines how to start publishing content online through the use of a blog. Chapter 7 shows how to share your digital photography with friends and family, allowing them to view your pictures online, as well as ordering prints.

The Components of a Website

In your experiences with the Internet you've likely visited several different websites. Some of the more popular websites in terms of the number of people that visit the site on a daily basis include Yahoo.com, Amazon.com, eBay.com, MSN.com, and others.

In order to visit a website, the computer being used must have an Internet connection. Virtually all computers in places of business have an Internet connection, while millions of home users connect to the Internet through services provided by companies such as AOL, MSN, Earthlink, Juno, or local Internet service providers.

> **NOTE**
>
> Companies that provide Internet connectivity—such as AOL, MSN, and others—are commonly referred to as *ISPs*, which stands for *Internet service provider*.

Visiting a website from an Internet-connected computer is a cinch. Simply open up a *web browser* and type in the *domain name* of the website into the web browser's Address bar.

> **NEW TERM**
>
> Each website has a unique *domain name*. To view a particular website, a user simply types in the domain name of the website she wants to visit in her browser's Address bar. We'll discuss the purpose of domain names in more detail shortly.

Figure 1.1 shows a screenshot of the MSN website when viewed through Internet Explorer.

Notice that Figure 1.1 has the browser's Address bar circled. To visit MSN's website simply enter the domain name of the site—www.msn.com—into the browser's Address bar. That's all you have to do.

Before you begin creating your own web pages, it is vital that you know of the basic components inherent to all websites. Specifically, all websites are made up from the following three components:

- ▶ **A Web Server**—A web server is an Internet-connected computer whose sole purpose is to provide a location for the web pages of a website and to handle incoming requests for these web pages.
- ▶ **A Domain Name**—A website's domain name is a unique identifier for a website, much like your mailing address is a unique identifier for your home. A website's domain name identifies the web server on which the site's web pages are located.
- ▶ **Web Pages**—A collection of files that make up the content of a website.

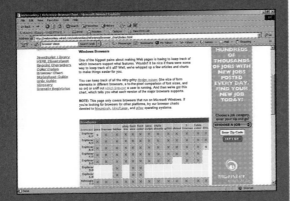

DOES YOUR WEBSITE LOOK RIGHT IN EVERY BROWSER?

Webmonkey is a particularly good site for tutorials on web building. We found a nice article and chart on what standards different browsers support. You may design and test your website using the browser on your computer. It may look fine to you, but what about all of your visitors and the browsers they're using? If you check out the browser statistics on www.counter.com, you'll find that 77% of people are using Microsoft Internet Explorer 6.x and 16% are using Internet Explorer 5.x. That at least narrows it down for you when you're trying to make sure your site can be viewed properly by most people. If you want to accommodate more people than that, pay attention to the standards on Mozilla, Netscape, Safari, and Opera, too.

Serving Web Pages with a Web Server

All websites are located on a special type of computer referred to as a *web server*, which is an Internet-accessible computer with that holds the contents of a specific website.

When visiting a website through a web browser, the web browser makes a *request* to the web server that hosts that particular website. The web server then returns the requested web page to the browser. Finally, the browser displays the web page, as was shown in Figure 1.1.

Figure 1.2 details this interaction from a high-level view.

If the details of this interaction seems a bit hazy, don't worry; you don't need to be concerned about the specifics. For now, just realize that the contents of a website reside on a remote computer that, like your computer, is connected to the Internet. The browser obtains the contents of the website you are visiting by making a request to the site's web server. The web server returns the web pages being requested, which are then displayed in the browser.

Understanding Website Domain Names

Did you know that there are literally *millions* of websites in existence? In order to visit a particular website from the list of millions, it is vital that all websites be uniquely identified in some manner. The way websites are uniquely identified is by their *domain name*.

FIGURE 1.1

The MSN website is displayed in the web browser.

FIGURE 1.2

Visiting a web page involves a request to a web server.

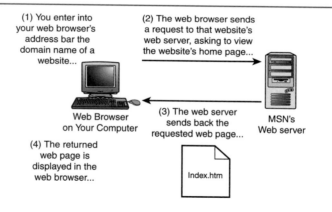

(1) You enter into your web browser's address bar the domain name of a website...

(2) The web browser sends a request to that website's web server, asking to view the website's home page...

Web Browser on Your Computer

(3) The web server sends back the requested web page...

MSN's Web server

(4) The returned web page is displayed in the web browser...

Index.htm

A domain name is, ideally, an easily remembered phrase, like eBay.com, Yahoo.com, or CNN.com. All domain names end with some sort of *extension*, which is a period followed by two or more letters. Most domain names end with extensions like .com, .net, or .org. Other extensions are available, though.

NOTE

Domain names provide a means to uniquely identify a website.

Web Pages, the Building Blocks of a Website

Web pages are the atomic pieces of a website; each website is a collection of web pages. When visiting a website with a web browser, what you are actually viewing is an individual web page.

On a website, each web page is, in actuality, a separate *file*. A file is a document that's stored on a computer. For example, if you use Microsoft Word to write a letter to your nephew, you can save the letter. This saved letter is referred to as a file.

You can request a particular web page from a website by typing the web page's URL into a web browser. You don't have to type in a URL to view a web page. As we saw earlier in Figure 1.1, typing in *just* the domain name of a website displays a web page as well. When typing in just the domain name of a website, a specific web page is automatically loaded—this page is referred to as the *home page*.

Getting Around a Website

A website is composed of a number of web pages. Each web page is uniquely identified by a URL. To visit a particular web page, you can enter the web page's URL in your browser's Address bar. However, as you know from surfing the Web on your own, rarely, if ever, do you take the time to enter a URL directly into the browser's Address bar.

An easier way to visit a particular web page is by first loading a website's home page, and then clicking on *hyperlinks* that take you to other pages on the site. Hyperlinks are clickable regions on a web page that, when clicked, whisk you to some other, specified web page. Hyperlinks are the means by which the web pages of a website are navigated.

TIP

Think of a website as a book, and a web page as a page in a book. When visiting a website you can navigate through the various web pages, just like when picking up a book you can flip around to different pages. You navigate through the pages of a book by thumbing through the pages; for a website, you navigate through its web pages by clicking on hyperlinks.

To demonstrate page navigation in a website, take a moment to visit the NBA's website at www.nba.com. As Figure 1.3 shows, this website (like all websites), has a number of hyperlinks. For example, you can click on the Players hyperlink for more information on the game's players, or the Standings hyperlink for a look at the current standings.

Clicking on the Players hyperlink whisks you to a new URL— http://www.nba.com/players/—which is shown in Figure 1.4. Notice that the Address bar in Figure 1.3 differs from that in Figure 1.4. In Figure 1.3, the Address bar reads http://www.nba.com, the domain name of the NBA website. After clicking on the Players hyperlink, we were taken to a different URL. The Address bar has been updated accordingly, illustrating that we are viewing a different web page.

NOTE

If you visit NBA.com while reading this book, the screenshots in Figures 1.3 and 1.4 may appear slightly different. That's because, unlike a book, a website is dynamic, allowing for its contents to be changed easily.

Figure 1.5 shows the interactions that take place between the web browser and the NBA.com web server when first visiting the NBA.com home page, and then when clicking on the Daily Glance hyperlink. (Again, if you do not fully understand this interaction, don't sweat it!)

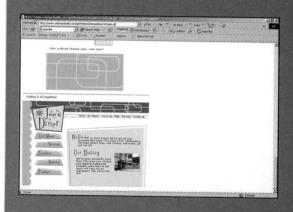

JUST GIVE ME A TEMPLATE!

What if you're not creative? What if you have no design education and experience at all? You still want a nice looking website that attracts visitors, and you have the skills to create it, but you need the look—the typefaces, the colors, the art. We just had to review Adam Polselli's site again for this very reason—he offers you an array of choices from simple chic to corporate to vintage and tells you step by step how to get the particular look that you want. After you read through his reasons for choosing elements to achieve his theme, he lets you click on a link called "Putting It All Together," where you'll see a bulleted list of typefaces he recommends, color schemes, shapes, borders, and photo finishes so that you can duplicate his design.

If you still want more than instructions to achieve a look, then you can buy HTML templates from websites. Try sites like Boxedart.com and designload.net, where you can buy full page templates or just buttons, art, and logos.

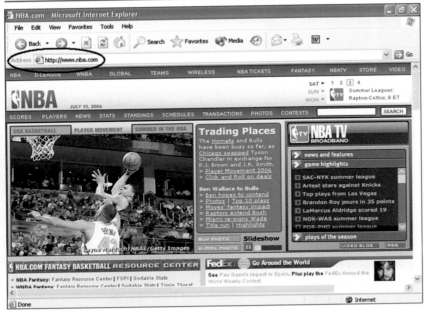

FIGURE 1.3
Visiting a web page
involves a request to a
web server.

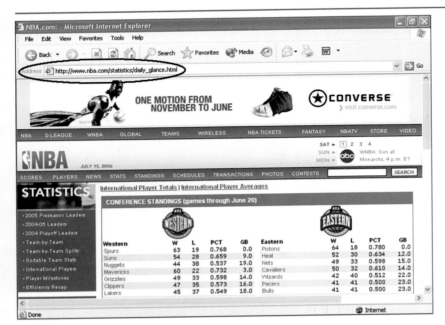

FIGURE 1.4
The Players web page is
displayed.

FIGURE 1.5

Each time a new web page is navigated to, the web browser requests the web page from the web server.

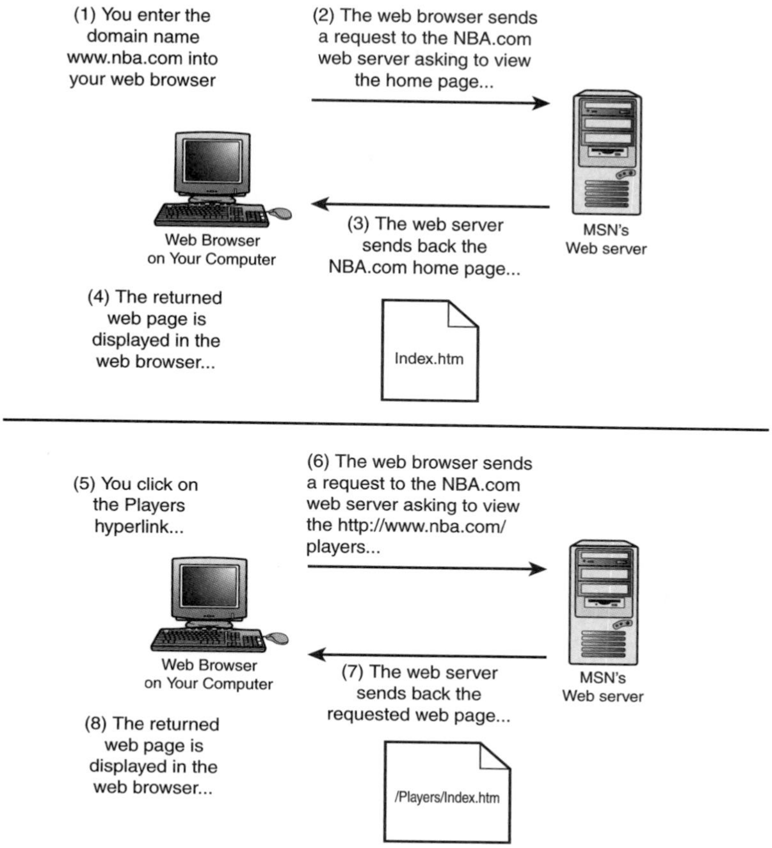

(1) You enter the domain name www.nba.com into your web browser

(2) The web browser sends a request to the NBA.com web server asking to view the home page...

Web Browser on Your Computer

(3) The web server sends back the NBA.com home page...

MSN's Web server

Index.htm

(4) The returned web page is displayed in the web browser...

(5) You click on the Players hyperlink...

(6) The web browser sends a request to the NBA.com web server asking to view the http://www.nba.com/players...

Web Browser on Your Computer

(7) The web server sends back the requested web page...

MSN's Web server

/Players/Index.htm

(8) The returned web page is displayed in the web browser...

Table 1.1 summarizes the core pieces of a website.

Table 1.1   Key Website Building Blocks

Building Block	Description
Web Server	A web server is an Internet-accessible computer that hosts one or more websites. When viewing a web page, your browser sends a request to the web server for the specified URL.
Website	A website is a collection of related web pages. Websites have a bevy of purposes: They can be used to share pictures, provide information, or even sell products. Each website is uniquely identified with a domain name.
Web Page	A web page can have a mix of text and graphics. A web page is like a single page in a book. Web pages can be linked to one another using hyperlinks, allowing the visitor to quickly jump from one web page to another.

IDEA GALLERY

http://www.useit.com/papers/webwriting/

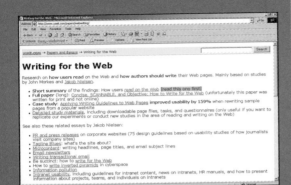

WRITING FOR YOUR SITE

"The most valuable of all talents is that of never using two words when one will do."
—Thomas Jefferson

Writing for the Web by Jakob Nielson is an older website, but still offers very relevant information about writing styles and effective communications with people. Although not the most attractive page, Jakob leads you to articles and other places to reference style rules, usability studies, guidelines for writing different kinds of text such as newsletters and press releases, as well as tips on writing headlines, subjects, and page titles that will get people's attention.

Building Web Pages Using Web Page Authoring Software Tools

Creating web pages is a simple task thanks to specially designed web page authoring software tools. These software tools allow you to visually construct a web page with a few points and clicks of the mouse. There are a number of different software packages out there that are designed to make creating web pages a snap. Table 1.2 lists some of the more popular ones, along with their price and a URL to learn more about the product.

Table 1.2	Popular Web Page Authoring Tools	
Name	Cost	For More Information...
Microsoft FrontPage	$199.00	http://www.microsoft.com/frontpage/
Macromedia DreamWeaver	$399.00	http://www.macromedia.com/software/dreamweaver/
Mozilla Composer	Free!	http://www.mozilla.org/

As you can tell by their prices, Microsoft FrontPage and Macromedia DreamWeaver are targeted toward the professional web developer. They are both world-class products that make building professional-looking websites an absolute breeze. Unfortunately, the price point for both of those products is a bit high for first-time web developers (like yourself).

Fortunately, there is a good, *free* web page authoring tool released by the Mozilla group, called Mozilla Composer.

NOTE

Mozilla is a not-for-profit organization established in 1998. The organization created and maintains a free web browser called Mozilla. The Mozilla web browser includes not just a web browser, but many other tools, including Composer, the web page authoring tool.

The CD accompanying this book contains the Mozilla browser associated tools. In order to use Mozilla Composer to create web pages, you will need to install the Mozilla browser on your computer. Once you have installed the Mozilla web browser you will be able to start using Mozilla Composer.

NOTE

The CD includes the most recent version of the Mozilla browser at the time of this book's writing, version 1.7.8. You may optionally download and install the most recent version of Mozilla from the Mozilla website—http://www.mozilla.org. If you do, though, realize that there may be some slight discrepancies between what you will see on your screen and the screenshots in this book.

Installing the Mozilla Browser

The CD accompanying this book includes the Mozilla web browser and Composer software, which you'll need to install on your computer to begin creating your first web page. To begin the installation, insert the CD into your computer. Next, go to My Computer and double-click on the CD-ROM drive. This will list the folders on the CD:

▸ Mozilla

▸ Templates

Open the Mozilla folder. Here you will find the file mozilla-win32-1.7.8.installer.exe. Double-click this file to begin the installation process. The installation process begins by displaying the Mozilla Setup – Welcome dialog box (shown in Figure 1.6).

FIGURE 1.6

The Mozilla installation welcome message.

Click the Next button to begin the installation. The second screen is the Software License Agreement screen, which provides the license for use of Mozilla and its associated products. Once you have read and agreed to this license, click the Accept button. Doing so will take you to the third screen, the Setup Type dialog box (shown in Figure 1.7). The Setup Type screen lets you determine what type of setup should be performed. Leave the default choice—Complete—selected, and click Next to continue.

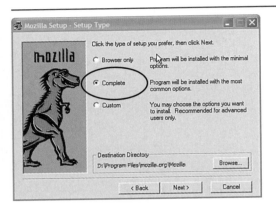

FIGURE 1.7
Choose to do a Complete installation.

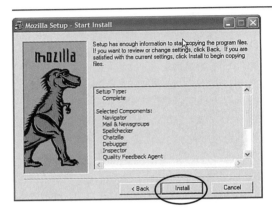

FIGURE 1.8
The final screen reviews the installation options.

The next screen asks you if you want to use Mozilla's Quick Launch option. Quick Launch adds an icon to the Windows taskbar, keeping Mozilla running even when you close it. This provides quicker startup times when you launch Mozilla. This option is unchecked by default, and I would encourage you to leave it unchecked unless you foresee yourself using the Mozilla browser regularly in place of Internet Explorer.

Once you have decided on the Quick Launch option, click Next to proceed to the final installation screen (shown in Figure 1.8). This final screen provides a summary of the components that will be installed.

Once you are ready to begin the actual installation, click the Install button. Over the next several minutes, Mozilla will be installed on your computer. Once it has completed installation, the Mozilla browser will automatically launch. With Mozilla installed, we are now ready to start using Composer, the web page editing software we'll be using throughout this book.

Starting Mozilla Composer

Once you have installed the Mozilla browser, you are ready to start using Mozilla Composer. To use Composer, you must first launch the Mozilla browser, if it is not running already. To launch Mozilla browser go to the Start menu, choose Programs, go to Mozilla, and select Mozilla.

Once the Mozilla browser has started, you can launch Composer by going to the Window menu in the browser and clicking on the Composer menu item. Alternatively, you can hit Ctrl and the 4 key on your keyboard simultaneously. Figure 1.9 shows a screenshot of the Mozilla browser and the Window menu.

BUILDING WEB PAGES USING WEB PAGE AUTHORING SOFTWARE TOOLS

Once you have selected to launch Composer, the Composer window should appear. Figure 1.10 shows a screenshot of the Composer window.

In the next section we'll examine how to use Composer to create a web page.

TIP

By installing Mozilla Composer, you are also installing a full-fledged web browser as well. The Mozilla web browser has many features not found in Internet Explorer. I would encourage you to try out the Mozilla browser—you might just like it better than Internet Explorer! To learn more about Mozilla's features check out http://mozilla.org/products/mozilla1.x/.

IDEA GALLERY

http://www.veer.com/

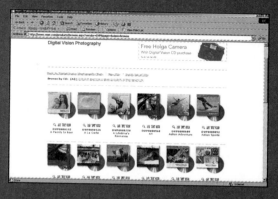

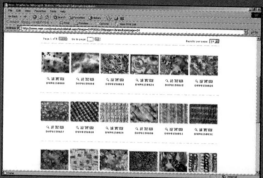

FONTS, IMAGES, PHOTOS, AND ILLUSTRATIONS FOR YOUR SITE

What if you want beautiful photos or illustrations for your site, but you're not an artist? Veer.com and plenty of other stock image sites offer great deals on images.

We liked Veer because they also print catalogs and offer them in PDF format from their website. Their catalogs are works of art themselves and can give you some great ideas for how to use images and type.

Here are a couple of tips to remember when looking for a stock image:

1. Royalty-free images are your best buy.
2. If you want the same look to your website, buy a CD of images that were designed to go together.

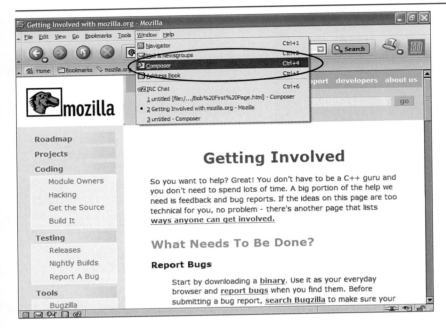

FIGURE 1.9

Launch Composer by selecting Composer from the Window menu.

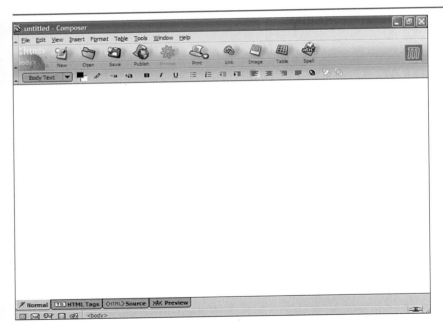

FIGURE 1.10

The Mozilla Composer window.

Creating a Web Page with Mozilla Composer

Creating web pages with Mozilla Composer is as easy and intuitive as writing a letter using a program such as Microsoft Word. Let's look at using Composer to build a simple web page, one that provides information about some fictitious individual. We'll start by just entering the content that we want to present in the web page, and will later come back and make the content appear more eye-pleasing.

> *"Creating web pages with Mozilla Composer is as easy and intuitive as writing a letter using a program such as Microsoft Word."*

To follow along, simply start Composer, if you haven't already. Recall that this can be accomplished by launching the Mozilla browser, going to the Window menu, and choosing the Composer option. (Refer back to Figure 1.9 for a screenshot of the Window menu in the Mozilla browser.)

Entering content into the web page is as simple as typing it in! The web page we'll be creating is about a fictitious fellow named Bob. In this page, Bob wants to share information about himself, including

- ▶ His age
- ▶ What he does for a living
- ▶ A bit about his wife and kids
- ▶ His hobbies
- ▶ Information about his pets

Start out by just typing in the information Bob wants to share with the world. Feel free to be creative and make up a bevy of interesting facts about Bob to share in this web page. I decided to enter the following for Bob:

Hello, you have reached my very first Web page! My name is Bob, I'm 34 years old and I live in Dallas, Texas.

I work as an instructor at a sky-diving school, teaching people how to jump out of planes. I've made over 400 jumps myself, and made my first jump back when I was a mere 12 years old!

I am married to my wife Irene, and we have seven lovely children: Bertha, Bobby-Joe, Jermain, Ted, Todd, Rod, and Lil' Elaine. Bertha's the biggest and oldest, and Lil' Elaine is the youngest (although not the smallest - Rod has that distinction).

For fun I like to bowl. I am in a league, and we play every Wednesday at the Bowlorama.

The joy of my life is my pet parrot, Mr. Polly. Mr. Polly has a large vocabulary, and is quite talkative, especially when the whole family sits down for dinner. Mr. Polly, believe it or not, has been on several jumps with me.

Figure 1.11 shows Composer after I have entered information about Bob.

Without a doubt, Bob's first web page is a bit of a disappointment. It doesn't look very exciting. Over the next several sections we'll examine how Composer allows you to spruce up the appearance of a web page. With a few simple steps you can radically improve the look and feel of a web page.

TIP

If you make a mistake when working with Composer—be it choosing an incorrect color, an incorrect font, mistyping, or whatever—you can undo your last action by going to the Edit menu and selecting Undo.

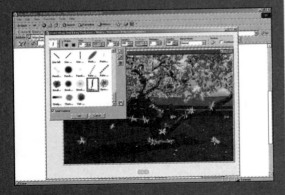

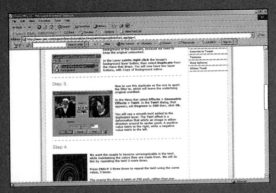

PAINT SHOP PRO

If you haven't heard about Paint Shop Pro yet, you should. This program that costs only $99 has almost as many features as Adobe Photoshop at a fraction of the price. It has effects packed into the program so that you can create halftones, 3D bubbles, different kinds of image distortions, tiled web page backgrounds and more. Their Community Gallery is especially cool. Users present some of their favorite projects that they completed in Paint Shop Pro. It's a great place to get ideas. And their Learning Center offers online tutorials for beginners. Download a trial version right from their website.

Changing the Font

By default, the text you type into Composer will be displayed using the web browser's default font. You can specify a specific font quite easily in Composer, though. To demonstrate this, let's have Bob's home page displayed in the Arial font.

To accomplish this, start by highlighting all of the text you've typed in thus far. To highlight the text you can go to the Edit menu and choose Select All, or, using the mouse, you can click and hold the button within the text and drag the mouse cursor to select a portion of the text. To change the selected text's font, go to the Format menu and choose the Font option. This will display a long list of available fonts, as shown in Figure 1.12. To follow along, choose the Arial font.

Figure 1.13 shows Composer after the font has been changed to Arial.

NOTE

Most professional web pages are displayed in one of three fonts: Arial, Times New Roman, or Verdana. Figure 1.14 shows the same sentence in these three different fonts.

FIGURE 1.11
Bob's first web page.

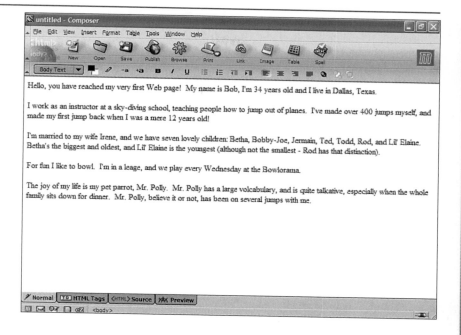

FIGURE 1.12
The Format menu's Font option lists the available fonts.

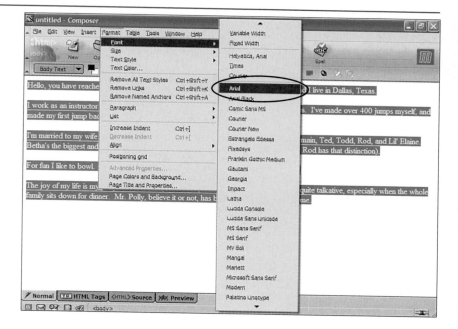

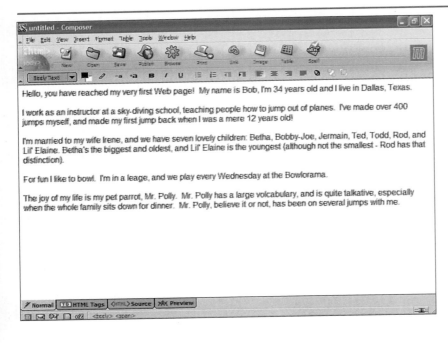

FIGURE 1.13

The text in Bob's web page is displayed in the Arial font.

This is an example of Arial.

This is an example of Times New Roman

This is an example of Verdana

FIGURE 1.14

Arial, Times New Roman, and Verdana are the three most popular fonts.

Making Text Bold, Italic, and Underlined

You can make text bold, italic, and underlined using the toolbar icons shown circled in Figure 1.15. To apply such formatting to a given piece of text, highlight the text and then click the appropriate icons.

TIP

To change the text for a portion of the document, use the mouse to select just the text whose font you want to change. Then go to the Format menu's Font option and select the font you want to change the selected text to.

For example, let's have Bob's children's names italicized. To accomplish this, use the mouse to select Bob's children's names. Once this text is selected, simply click the Italic icon (the *I* in the toolbar), and the text will become italicized.

Also, let's add a brief title before each paragraph, where each title is made bold. Figure 1.16 shows Composer after the boldfaced paragraph titles have been added and the children's names italicized.

TIP

You are not limited to making text only bold or italicized or underlined. You can make text both bold and italic, or both italic and underlined, or any other combination of the three.

Changing the Colors

Composer allows you to easily specify the foreground color for text, and the background color for a web page. To set the foreground color, simply select the text whose color you want to change, and then go to the Format menu and choose the Text Color menu option. Choosing this option will display the Text Color dialog box, which is shown in Figure 1.17.

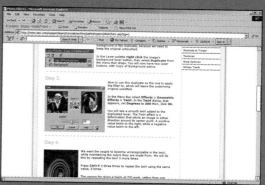

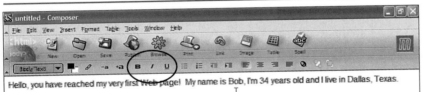

FIGURE 1.15

These toolbar icons allow you to make text bold, italic, and underlined.

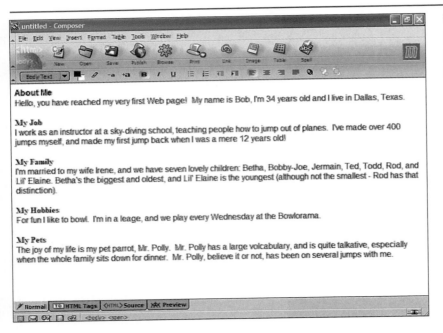

FIGURE 1.16

Some bold and italic formatting has been applied.

This dialog box allows you to choose a color from a palette of colors. Upon selecting a color and clicking the OK button, the dialog box will close and the selected text's foreground color will change to the specified color. Take a moment to alter the foreground color of some text in Bob's web page.

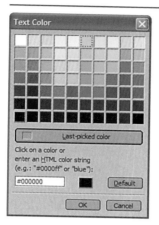

FIGURE 1.17

The Text Color dialog box allows you to select the text's color.

The web page's background color can be changed by going to the Format menu and choosing the Page Colors and Backgrounds option. This will display the Page Colors and Backgrounds dialog box (shown in Figure 1.18). To change the page's background color, select the Use custom colors radio button and then click on the Background button. This will display the Text Color dialog box shown in Figure 1.17. After choosing a color and clicking OK in both dialog boxes, you will be returned to Composer and the background color will have changed to the specified color.

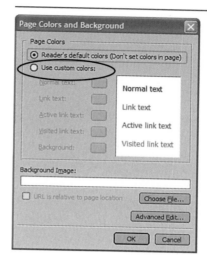

FIGURE 1.18

This dialog box allows you to change the background color of the web page.

TIP

When specifying colors, be sure that the background and foreground colors contrast so that the text is readable. If you choose a dark text color on a dark background, or a light text color on a light background, visitors to your web page won't be able to read the text!

Some examples of bad color choices include yellow text on a white background and blue text on a black background.

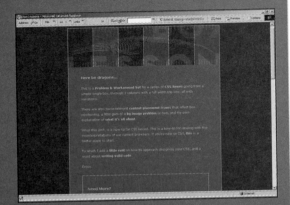

WHO SAYS A GOOD SITE HAS TO BE COLORFUL?

We picked this site for two reasons. First of all, it's a clean, interesting, and simple design that looks great without color. Second, it's a useful site for those of you just learning how to build websites in that it gives you tips and advice on CSS—Cascading Style Sheets.

So many sites are filled with jumbles of color and bright flashing animations that it's hard to know where to click. This site contains only shades of gray with header graphics contained at the top of each page and a simple one-column design. It's very elegant.

This site's designer does a lot of nice things to keep his navigation simple for his users. He adds links within his paragraphs to illustrate his points or send you to other useful sites. This site reads like an instructional book or guide. Unlike some commercial sites that give you a million places to jump from just one page, this designer keeps the messages simple and allows you to stay focused on one topic at a time.

Positioning Text

Like with a word processor, Composer allows you to position text in one of four ways:

- ▶ Left-aligned
- ▶ Center-aligned
- ▶ Right-aligned
- ▶ Justified

To specify the positioning, simply select the text you wish to position and then choose the appropriate positioning icon from the toolbar. Figure 1.19 shows the text-alignment toolbar icons circled.

To practice text positioning, take a moment to right-align all of the paragraph titles (About Me, My Job, and so on). To right-align the About Me title, simply select the text and then click the right-align toolbar icon. Repeat this process for all paragraph titles on the page.

Figure 1.20 shows Composer after the right-aligning has been performed.

Saving the Web Page

There are many more formatting options in Composer, and we will examine these in detail when we start building full-blown websites. The goal of the past few sections was to introduce you to some of the more basic formatting options Composer provides, and to hammer home the concept that formatting in Composer is synonymous to formatting text in a word processor.

FIGURE 1.19

These toolbar icons allow for positioning of text.

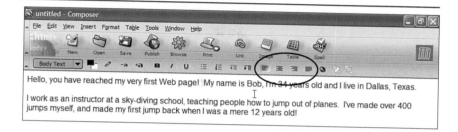

FIGURE 1.20

The paragraph titles are now right-aligned.

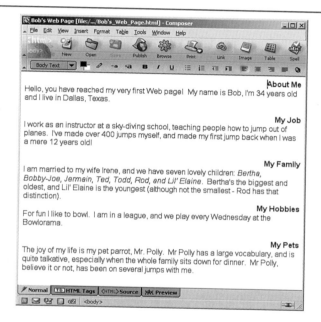

"There are many formatting options in Composer, and we will examine these in detail when we start building full-blown websites."

Now that you have completed Bob's first web page, save it. To save the web page, go to the File menu and choose the Save option. This will display a dialog box prompting us for the *title* for this web page.

NEW TERM

All web pages have a *title* associated with them. The title is what is displayed in the web browser's title bar when the page is visited.

Choose a title, such as "Bob's First Web Page" and click OK. Next, you will be prompted for where to save the file. You can save it anywhere on your computer you'd like, such as in the My Documents folder, on the Desktop, or in a custom folder. You can open this web page for further editing at a future time by starting Composer, going to the File menu, and then choosing the Open option.

At this point, the web page is saved only on your computer. There is no way that your grandmother in Toledo could visit this web page through her web browser. In order to make this web page accessible to anyone with an Internet connection, we will need to create a website and then copy this file to the web server that hosts our website. This involves a number of steps, which we'll examine in detail in the next chapter.

Summary

With the completion of this chapter you've taken your first step in your journey to create websites. This chapter was a big first step, covering many important facets of websites, web pages, and web page authoring tools.

This chapter began by looking at the three things all websites have:

▶ A web server to return the requested web pages to the requesting web browsers

▶ A domain name, to uniquely identify the website

▶ Web pages, which make up the building blocks of a website

A web server is a computer where a website's web pages reside. It is this web server that is queried when a user visits the website through a web browser. The domain name is a unique identifier for a website. To visit the home page for a particular website, simply enter the domain name in your web browser's Address bar. Finally, a website is composed of one to many web pages. Each web page is, in actuality, a file residing on the web server. Web pages contain HTML markup that specifies how their content should be displayed in a web browser.

In this chapter you also saw how to use Mozilla Composer to create a simple web page. Composer enables you to create and edit web pages just like you would work with documents in any word processor program. Before you can start using Composer, though, you first need to install the Mozilla software located on this book's accompanying CD.

In the next chapter, "Creating a Website," we'll take a deeper look at the communication interactions involved between a web browser and a web server. We'll also look at how to get started creating a website, which involves finding a web host provider and registering a domain name. Finally, we'll see how to upload web pages from your computer onto your public website's web server. You'll find all this and more in the next chapter!

CHAPTER 2

Creating a Website

In the previous chapter you examined how to use Composer to create your first web page. After creating the web page, you saved the web page to a folder on your computer. While storing the web page on your computer allows you to easily update the web page at some time in the future, it does not permit others to view your web page via a web browser. That is, when the web page is stored just on your computer, you are the only person who can view your web page.

In order to share a web page with the world, you need to create a *website*.

A *website* is a computer with a permanent connection to the Internet, whose web pages are accessible to anyone with an Internet connection. Creating a website involves three steps:

1. Contact a *web host provider* and obtain a public website.
2. Register a *domain name*, such as www.MyFirstWebSite.com, and have the domain name registered with the website.
3. Upload your web pages to the public website.

Once you accomplish these three steps, your web pages will be able to be viewed by anyone connected to the Internet! As discussed in the previous chapter, people will be able to visit your website by simply opening a web browser and typing your website's domain name into the Address bar.

> *"In order to share a web page with the world, you need to create a website."*

In this chapter you will learn how to accomplish each of these three steps. If you follow along, by the end of this chapter you will have a publicly available website that you can share with your friends, family, and customers!

Finding a Web Host Provider

The first step in creating a public website is finding a *web host provider*. A web host provider is a company that offers a computer that is connected to the Internet 24 hours a day, seven days a week. This computer functions as a web server—that is, it does nothing but wait for incoming requests from remote web browsers. Upon receiving a request, it returns the requested web page.

There are multitudes of web host providers, from small one-man companies to Fortune 100 companies publicly traded on the stock market. Costs, too, run the gamut, all the way from free to several thousand dollars per month.

Given the sheer number of web host providers, finding a web host provider is not challenging in the least. Simply go to any search engine and type "web hosting company" into the search box. Such a search at Google.com provides an estimated 6.7 million matching results!

Another approach is to use one of the many websites that serve as a "white pages" of web hosting companies. Sites such as TopHosts (www.tophosts.com), HostIndex (www.hostindex.com), and HostSearch (www.hostsearch.com) provide a searchable index of thousands of web hosting companies around the world.

If you want to save the hassle of searching for a web host provider through a search engine or a host index-type site, consider asking your Internet service provider (ISP) if they offer web hosting.

NOTE

Your ISP is the company that provides your computer with Internet access. Common ISPs are companies such as AOL, Earthlink, MSN, and many phone companies, such as SBC.

TIP

ISPs often make for ideal web host providers because oftentimes a web hosting account is included in the monthly price paid for Internet service. With other web hosting companies, you'll need to pay a monthly fee for the services provided.

Important Web Hosting Metrics

When researching web hosting companies, you'll find that they all toss around various technical sounding facts, like, "We offer 250MB of disk space and a monthly transfer limit of 2GB!" To help make sense of this technical and marketing mumbo-jumbo, let's take a moment to examine some of the common technical benchmarks used.

Disk Space

Oftentimes web hosting companies limit you to storing only a certain amount of data on the web server. This number can range from web host to web host, but typically a web host will allow you to store anywhere from 10 megabytes (MB) to 250MBs on the web server.

The amount of web space you'll need depends on what you plan on storing on your website. If you plan on just having web pages and some pictures, 20MB should be more than enough. Realize that each picture taken from a digital camera can consume anywhere from 50 kilobytes (KB) to 250KB, depending on the quality and settings of the camera. (A megabyte is approximately 1,000 kilobytes.)

So, assuming your digital camera takes pictures that are 250KB, the upper bound, you could store four pictures per megabyte. If you wanted to share, say, 25 pictures, then you'd need 6,250KB, or 6.25MB. As you can see, a 20MB account is usually sufficient for most peoples' websites, but if you anticipate posting large amounts of pictures, or other files that are exceptionally large in size, you will want to choose a web host that provides your anticipated disk space needs.

TIP

If you plan on sharing a large number of pictures, consider using a free image sharing service like SnapFish. With these image sharing sites you can upload your digital pictures and invite friends and family to view the images and, optionally, order prints. Chapter 7, "Sharing Images Online with SnapFish," provides a detailed look at posting your pictures online with SnapFish.

If you plan on creating your own website using the templates in this book's accompanying CD then you will need to use a web hosting provider in order to have your website accessible on the Internet. If, however, you plan on building your site using one of the web applications discussed in Chapters 5, 6, or 7, your site and its content will be hosted on these web servers of the company whose services you utilize.

For example, in Chapter 5, "Selling Products with an eBay Store," you'll learn how to sell inventory through eBay Stores. eBay Stores is a web application provided by eBay that makes it easy to list products for sale and collect payment from interested buyers for a small percentage of the sale. With an eBay Store, the web pages that comprise your website are automatically created by eBay and hosted on eBay.com's web servers. In this case you don't need to worry about finding a web hosting provider since eBay acts as the hosting provider.

Monthly Transfer Limit

Every time someone visits a web page from a website, the website must transfer the contents of the web pages, and any pictures on the web page, to the requesting web browser. The more data transferred from a web server, the more cost is incurred by the web host provider. Therefore, to keep costs down, many web host providers specify some sort of monthly transfer cap for a website.

"For small personal sites, a 2GB transfer limit is typically more than enough."

> **NOTE**
> The monthly transfer limit is sometimes referred to as the *monthly bandwidth*.

Typical monthly transfer limits are in the range of 2 gigabytes (GB) to 10GB. (One gigabyte is approximately 1,000 megabytes.) Some web hosts use the monthly transfer limit as a *hard limit*. That is, if the monthly bandwidth exceeds the limit, the website is shut down for the remainder of the month. Other web hosts use the limit as a *soft limit*, meaning that after the monthly limit is exceeded, a specified cost per exceeded GB is tacked on to the monthly web hosting service fees. And other websites don't impose a monthly transfer limit at all.

For small personal sites, a 2GB transfer limit is typically more than enough. To put things in perspective, consider that your website has content totaling 10MB of disk space. Assume that each visitor ends up viewing on average 2MB worth of pictures and other content. Now, assume that you have 250 visitors per month; that knocks the monthly bandwidth up to 500MB, or 0.5GB.

Of course if you expect a deluge of visitors, 2GB might not be enough. If you think your site will be heavily trafficked, or you plan on hosting content that is large in file size (such as home videos, MP3s of songs you've written, or other large files), you might want to choose a web hosting company that does not impose a monthly bandwidth limit.

FTP Support

At some point you will need to move the web pages you've create with Composer from your local machine to the web host company's web server. A very common means for transferring files from one computer to another over the Internet is *FTP*. FTP stands for *File Transfer Protocol*, and is the de facto protocol for transferring files between remote computers. Composer uses the FTP protocol to upload files from your local computer to the host's web server. Therefore, it is vital that the web hosting company you choose to go with supports FTP access.

> "...A number of free web hosting companies, such as GeoCities (www.geocities.com), offer a free website, but require that you pay a nominal monthly fee for FTP access."

Virtually all web host companies provide FTP access. The thing to watch out for, though, is that a number of free web hosting companies, such as GeoCities (www.geocities.com), offer a free website, but require that you pay a

nominal monthly fee for FTP access. Therefore, make sure that the plan you choose to go with does include FTP support so that you can transfer your web pages from Composer to the web server.

Table 2.1: Important Web Host Terms	
Metric	**Description**
Disk Space	Web hosts typically limit the number of web pages, images, and other files that you can have on your website. If you plan on storing many large images on your site, be sure to choose a web hosting plan with adequate disk space.
Monthly Transfer Limit	To help manage data transfer costs, web hosting companies typically place a limit on your site's bandwidth. For small websites, 2 gigabytes of monthly bandwidth are typically more than sufficient. However, if you're planning on building a widely trafficked site, make sure you choose a web hosting plan with sufficient transfer limits.
FTP Access	In order to upload your web pages from Composer to your web server, the web hosting company will need to provide FTP access.

Picking a Web Hosting Company

Once you have researched a variety of web hosting companies, it is time to pick one of them and sign up! Web host companies typically charge an initial setup fee along with a recurring monthly fee.

Most large ISPs provide web hosting support along with the paid Internet connectivity, so you might first want to check with your ISP and see what they can offer web hosting-wise.

Before you sign up with a web hosting company I would strongly encourage you to first check—and then double-check—that the company provides FTP support for the plan you are signing up for. Remember, FTP support is needed so that Composer can be used to upload the web pages.

Registering a Domain Name

Recall from Chapter 1 that to visit a website, you just need to type the website's domain name into the browser's Address bar. If you want a domain name for your website, such as www.MyFirstWebSite.com, you'll need to register the domain name you want and configure the domain name to point to the web hosting company's web server.

> **NOTE**
>
> Realize that you do not need to associate a domain name with your website. If you do not, though, your website's address will be something like: http://www.WebHostCompanyName.com/YourWebSiteName. With a domain name, however, your website will be accessible by something more personalized, like http://www.YourWebSiteName.com.

To register a domain name, perform the following two steps:

1. Choose and then purchase an available domain name.

2. Configure the domain name so that it references the correct website.

Over the next two sections you'll see how to accomplish these two steps. Don't worry if these sound like daunting tasks; as you'll learn shortly, they both are relatively simple to perform, even for the computer layperson.

> **TIP**
>
> If you are concerned about performing these two steps on your own, understand that most web hosting companies will perform these steps for you for free or for a nominal charge. If you'd rather leave this to a professional, simply ask your web host if they can register a domain name for you.

Choosing and Buying a Domain Name

When registering a domain name, you can only choose a domain name that has not been registered by someone else. That is, you cannot take an existing domain name—say www.microsoft.com—and register that domain name, having it point to your website. So, the first step in registering a domain name is finding and selecting an available domain name.

Domain names can be purchased from a variety of domain name registrars. A *domain name registrar* is a company that is sanctioned by the Internet Corporation for Assigned Names and Numbers (ICANN) to allow registration of domain names. There are dozens of such companies available, varying in price and quality of service. A complete list can be found at http://www.icann.org/registrars/accredited-list.html.

NOTE

When purchasing a domain name, you are not buying the domain name outright. Rather, you are essentially leasing the domain name for a specified period of time (between one and ten years). After this period of time has ended, as the registrant of the domain name you can re-register the domain name for another period of time, or you can release the domain name, returning it to the pool of available domain names.

A common registrar used is Network Solutions (www.networksolutions.com). At the time of this writing, they charge $34.99 to register the domain name for one year, or less per year if registering for multiple years. Before a domain name can be registered, though, it must be available.

To determine if a domain name is available, start by going to any domain name registrar company's website, such as www.networksolutions.com. These companies will typically have a search box on their site to search for available domain names. Figure 2.1 shows the Network Solutions homepage. Notice that there is a text box that lets you enter a domain name, along with what extensions you want to search on (.com, .org, .net, .info, and so forth).

Upon searching for a domain name, you will see whether or not the domain names are available. If they are, you can register for them, choosing how long to register the domain name. If the name is already taken, a list of similar domain names is suggested. Figure 2.2 shows the results of a search for the domain name ScottsFirstWebSite searching on extensions .com, .org, and .net.

IDEA GALLERY

http://www.internic.net/whois.html

I'M READY FOR MY OWN DOMAIN NAME

If you're starting a business online or you want to own a domain name, you'll need to know which ones are already taken. InterNIC runs a page called WhoIs, where you can type in a domain that you want to own and find out if it's in use or for sale. As an example, let's say that we might want to create a domain for this book. If you type in "createwebsite.com" into the WhoIs search window, you'll find that Tucows Inc. owns that particular domain name. They bought it in August 2001, and the name expires in August 2006. Happy searching.

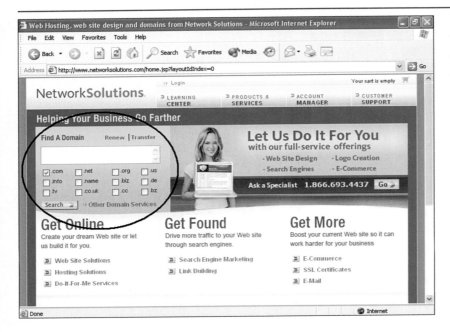

FIGURE 2.1
The Network Solutions home page lets you search for available domain names.

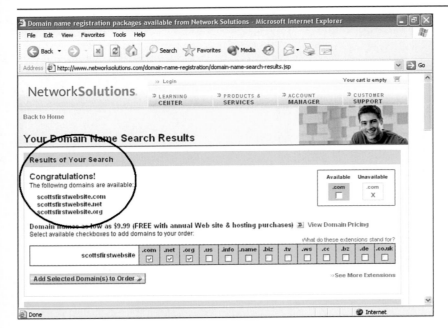

FIGURE 2.2
Searching on a domain name returns a list of available domain names, along with similar domain names and extensions.

To register the checked domain names, simply click the Continue button. This will take you through a checkout process, where you specify the duration of the domain name registration, and provide your credit card number for payment.

Configuring the Domain Name

Sometime during the domain name registration process, you will be asked to provide the *IP address* for the *name servers* you want the domain name to point to. While these terms may sound like Greek to you, the web hosting company is familiar with these terms, and can help you out. Simply ask the web hosting company what name server IP addresses to use—they'll provide you with, typically, two IP addresses that you can enter as the primary and secondary name server addresses. (An IP address is a number of the form XXX.XXX.XXX.XXX, where XXX is a number between 0 and 255.)

NOTE

Realize that there can be a 24- to 72-hour delay after registering and configuring a domain name and before the domain name officially points to the appropriate web server. That means that it can take a few days after registering your domain name before anyone can visit your website by directly entering the domain name into their web browser.

TIP

Remember, if you get overwhelmed with registering the domain name and specifying the name servers, you can always ask your web hosting company to perform them for you.

At this point you have chosen a web hosting provider and, perhaps, registered a domain name. The only piece of the puzzle that's left is adding web pages, images, and other files to the web server. This is accomplished by uploading the web pages we create in Composer to the web server.

Uploading Web Pages from Composer to Your Website

In order to upload web pages from Composer to your public website, you will first need to procure some information from your web hosting company. The pertinent information, which was likely emailed to you when you signed up with the web hosting company, is

▶ The FTP server to upload your files

▶ Your username and password to access the FTP server

Armed with this information, you are ready to upload a web page from Composer to your website.

First, you must have a web page to upload. In Chapters 3 and 4 you'll be examining two different website templates. Each template is composed of a series of web pages. To create a website, you'll take the template from the CD, customize it for your site, and then upload the

LOOKING FOR A WEB HOSTING SITE— SHOP AROUND

There are some great sites out there for hosting your website. We found SecureWebs to have a range of services and an online catalog of features. Shop around for the best deal and the types of services that you want. You may only need a small amount of space for a family or hobby website, which you can usually get from your Internet provider. Most accounts offer FTP access and a 50–100 MB of space for your own little website. But if you want to create a larger website, especially one that involves selling products or services, you might want to let a hosting site do most of the work for you. These sites take care of mass emailing, shopping carts, online catalogs, and newsletters for you. They also have security for your site, which can be difficult to program by yourself if you're a beginner. They have firewalls to prevent hackers from destroying your website as well as SSL (Secure Sockets Layer) that allows your visitors to perform transactions in a secure environment.

modified template to your website. Since you've yet to examine these templates, for now upload the practice web page you created (and saved) in Chapter 1. Start by opening the web page we created in Chapter 1 by launching Composer, and then going to the File menu and choosing the Open File menu option.

Once you have opened this web page, your screen should look similar to Figure 2.3.

Now, upload this web page to your public web server. To do so, go to the File menu and choose the Publish menu option (see Figure 2.4).

This will display the Publish Page dialog box. The Publish Page dialog box has two tabs: Publish and Settings. When first publishing a page to a public website, you will be taken to the Settings tab (shown in Figure 2.5), where you are prompted for the website's name, its FTP server, the web address, and the FTP server login information (username and password).

In the Publishing address text box, enter the name of the FTP server your web host provider told you to use. In the HTTP address of your home page text box, enter the URL for your website. In the User name and Password text boxes, enter the username and password you were given to access the FTP server. Once you have provided this information once, you will not need to enter it again.

FIGURE 2.3

The first web page we created back in Chapter 1.

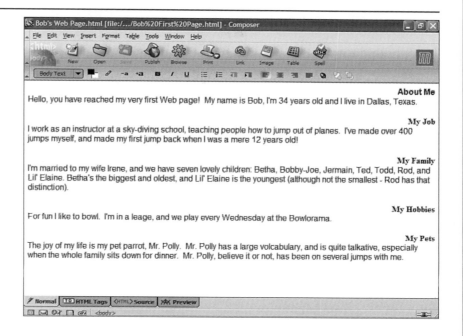

FIGURE 2.4

To upload a web page, choose File, Publish.

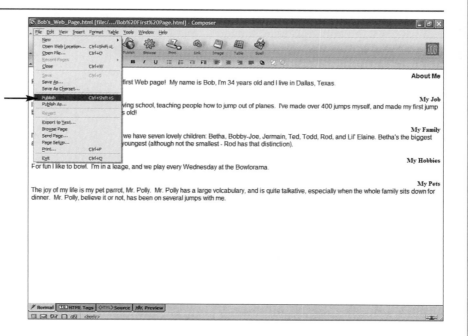

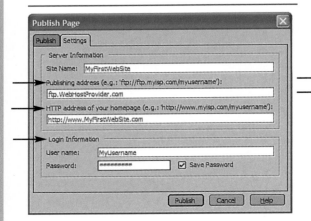
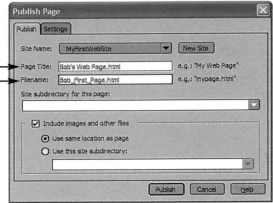

FIGURE 2.5
Specify FTP server settings in the Publish Page dialog box's Settings tab.

FIGURE 2.6
Set the web page's title and filename in the Publish Page dialog box's Publish tab.

Upon entering this information into the Settings tab, click on the Publish tab. This tab, shown in Figure 2.6, allows you to optionally specify the web page's title, and requires that you specify a filename for the web page. Remember from our discussions in Chapter 1 that web pages are actually stored as files on the web server. Therefore, you need to provide a filename for this web page. For the web pages you'll be creating throughout this book, be sure to name your files with the extension .htm or .html.

After providing a title and filename click the Publish button. This will display the Publishing dialog box, and report on the status of the web page upload. Figure 2.7 shows the Publishing dialog box after the file has been successfully uploaded.

NOTE
Recall from Chapter 1 that the title of a web page appears in the title of the web browser when visiting the page.

FIGURE 2.7
Bob's web page has been successfully uploaded.

NOTE

If you get an error when trying to publish a web page, the error may be due to an incorrect FTP server name, or invalid login credentials. Go to File, Publish As, and re-enter the FTP location and FTP credentials in the Settings tab. If you still experience problems, contact your web hosting provider for further assistance.

Once you have uploaded the web page, you can visit the web page through a web browser. To do so, enter into the browser's Address bar the URL to your website—either the domain name, if you have one, or the URL provided by your web hosting company, such as http://www.webhostingcompany.com/YourWeb Site—followed by the name of the web page you uploaded. So, to visit Bob's web page, which was named Bob's_Web_Page.html, you could visit the page by entering http://www.YourDomainName.com/ Bob's_Web_Page.html or http://www.webhostprovider.com/YourWebSite/ Bob's_Web_Page.html. Figure 2.8 shows a screenshot of visiting Bob's web page on my public website, whose domain name is http://www.ScottAndJisun.com.

IDEA GALLERY

http://www.searchenginewatch.com/reports/article.php/3099931

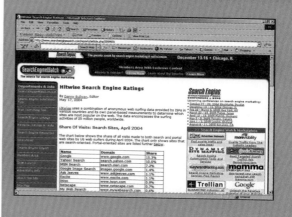

HOW DO PEOPLE FIND YOUR SITE?

In a previous sidebar, we mentioned web robots and crawlers that search engines use to detect sites on the Internet. If you want to know which search engines are most popular, go to Search Engine Watch, and you'll discover where most people go to find sites. The majority of searchers, 15%, go to Google.com to look for websites. If you want to get noticed or advertise to your customers, the majority of your time and resources should go into making sure that Google knows your site and lists it properly. On the other hand, more people visit the Yahoo.com portal every day—29%. It's a good home page for any browser because it offers up-to-date news, a link to email, stock reports, and other useful links. Find out from Search Engine Watch how to submit your site to these portals and optimize your listing.

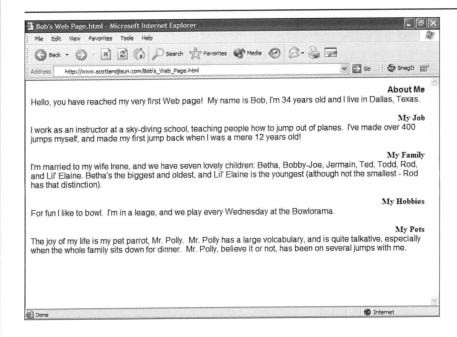

FIGURE 2.8

Bob's website is now online, accessible by anyone with an Internet connection!

Building a Website from a Template

The CD accompanying this book contains web pages for two templates. When creating your own websites, you'll want to start with one of these templates, customizing the template's pages for your site's particular content. Chapters 3 and 4 discuss various tips for modifying these templates. For now, it is important to understand the process you'll need to take in order to modify a template on the CD.

"The CD accompanying this book contains web pages for two templates. When creating your own websites, you'll want to start with one of these templates, customizing the template's pages for your site's particular content."

To start, you'll want to copy the template's files from the CD to your computer's hard drive. From there, you can use Composer to tweak each template file, saving the changes. Also, you may want to include additional pages for your site, using the provided template's look and feel. To summarize the process, when building a site from a template, you'll want to perform the following steps:

1. Create a new folder on your computer's hard drive.

2. Copy all of the template's files from the CD to the folder created in step 1.

3. Launch Composer. Recall that this is accomplished by running Mozilla, and then going to the Window menu and choosing the Composer menu option.

4. Open one of the template files copied to the folder in step 2. You can also add a new web page to your site by creating a page in Composer based on the template. We'll discuss how to do this in the "Customizing the Template" section later in this chapter.

5. Customize the template file's contents for your website.

6. Save the changes made to the template file.

You'll want to repeat steps 4 through 6 for each of the files in the template. Once you have customized and saved each of the pages in the template, the final step is to publish the website to a web server, so that anyone with an Internet connection can view your site. The publishing process is described at the end of each of the remaining chapters.

NOTE

In Chapters 5 through 7 you'll learn how to use existing web applications to sell items, publish content, and share pictures online. For these chapters you won't need to FTP web pages to a web server, since the web pages will be automatically created and hosted by the web application service provider.

Summary

In this chapter you learned the steps necessary for creating a public website, which include

► Finding a web host provider

► Registering a domain name (optional)

► Uploading web pages from Composer to the web server

As discussed, there are innumerous web host providers available that you can chose from, varying in price, service, and features offered. Thankfully there are entire websites—like TopHosts.com and HostIndex.com—that act as search engines for web host providers. Rather than using a separate web hosting company, your Internet service provider (ISP) might also provide web hosting capabilities for free. When selecting a web hosting company be sure to choose one whose disk space and monthly transfer limits meet your site's needs, and one that provides FTP access.

After choosing a company to host your website, you can optionally register a domain name, giving your website a personalized, memorable name, like www.YourWebSite.com. A domain name can be leased for one to ten years using a domain name registrar, like Network Solutions. When registering a domain name you'll need to know the IP address of your web host company's nameservers. This information associates your domain name with your website. (For more information on this process, refer to the "Understanding How the Internet Works" section in the Bonus Material chapter available on this book's CD.)

Once you have selected a web host provider you can upload web pages from your personal computer to your website, so that anyone with

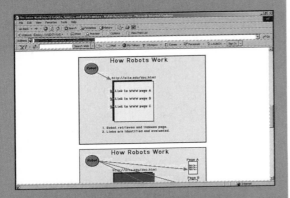

HOW SEARCH ENGINES FIND YOUR WEBSITE

Ever wonder how websites pop up in search engine results from Yahoo or Google? The article "The Inner Workings of Robots, Spiders, and Web Crawlers" by Lee Underwood explains how search engines find new websites and what you can do to help spiders and robots list your site properly. The article tells you how to create metatags that gives instructions to the robots and keywords for people looking for your type of site. Don't miss the bottom of the article, where the author gives you links to important robot validators, databases of Web robots, and places to stop spambots.

an Internet connection can view your pages. If you followed along in acquiring a web hosting provider, registering a domain name, and uploading files, you should now have a publicly accessible website that can be visited by anyone in the world with an Internet connection!

With the information covered in this chapter and the previous one, you have enough knowledge to start creating your own website! Chapters 3 and 4 explore different templates that you can quickly and easily modify to build different types of websites!

CHAPTER 3

Creating a Family/Personal Website

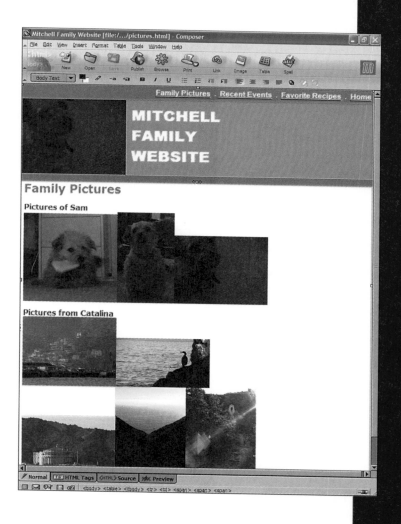

The book's first two chapters looked at the pieces that make up the Internet and websites, and showed how to create simple web pages with Composer. At this point you're ready to examine how to use Composer to build a complete website. While you can create a website from scratch, it's much easier and quicker to start working with a *website template*. A website template, often referred to as just a *template*, is a collection of generic, pre-made web pages that can be easily customized to create a specific site.

When designing websites, designers typically start with an appropriate template and then tailor the template's pages accordingly. Throughout this book you'll be examining four different templates, starting with a template for a family/personal website.

Examining the Family/Personal Template

Friends and families today are increasingly distant, spread around the country and world. Fortunately, keeping your families and friends up-to-date with what's going on in your life is made remarkably easier with a family/personal website, which provides family and friends a one-stop location to catch up on your life. Most family/personal websites have similar features: pictures of the family or person the website is about, a list of recent happenings, and important upcoming dates, such as anniversaries or birthdates.

As you can see in Figure 3.1, the family/personal website template provided with the book's accompanying CD offers a template that contains the following pages:

- ▶ A homepage that gives a brief description of the site and has links to the other web pages

- ▶ A photo gallery index page, which provides a list of links to various family pictures

- ▶ A recent news page, which lists the latest family events

- ▶ A list of recipes for the family's favorite recipes

In this chapter you'll examine how you can tailor the family/personal template. As you'll see, it's quite easy to take the provided template and change the look and feel, as well as add and remove content. For example, the pages provided in the template are just a few of many potential web pages that you may want to add to your family/personal website. Other potential pages include

- ▶ The scores from a child's soccer games.

- ▶ Information about children's after-school activities, such as cheerleading or debate.

- ▶ Any other bit of information your extended family or friends might care to hear about!

In the "Customizing the Template" section you'll see just how easy it is to add new pages to your family/personal website.

Before you can start customizing the template, you'll first need to understand how to start working with the template files. Essentially, you'll need to copy the template's files from the CD to your computer's hard drive.

FIGURE 3.1

The family/personal website template.

This chapter concludes with a discussion on how to *publish* your website, once you have tailored the template. Publishing a website involves copying the web pages from your computer to the web server computer where your public website is hosted. As we'll see, Composer makes this process a simple one.

Customizing the Template

The family/personal website template shown in Figure 3.1 provides bare-bone web pages that you can easily add to and customize to create your own unique family/personal website. If you like the look and feel of the template, all that's left to do is to customize the template's content, replacing the current text with the text pertinent to you and your family, and the image in the upper-left corner with an image of your own choosing.

"When working with the template, you may find that you want to customize certain aspects. ... Fortunately, Composer makes customizing the template quick, fun, and easy."

NOTE

Recall that to customize a template you need to copy the template files from the book's accompanying CD to your computer's hard drive. The "Building a Website from a Template" section in Chapter 2, "Creating a Website," provides more details on this process.

When working with the template, you may find that you want to customize certain aspects. For example, you might want to change the template's font, or alter the text or background colors. You might want to add additional web pages to the template, such as a web page that lists important dates (anniversaries, birthdays, and so on). You might want to remove pages from the template; perhaps you don't want a favorite recipes page.

Fortunately, Composer makes customizing the template in any of these ways quick, fun, and easy. In this section we'll be examining a myriad of ways to customize your template. When working with the template files, keep the following two things in mind:

▶ Composer is like any other word processor. If you want to customize the page by centering some text, for example, simply select the text to center and click on the Center icon in the Toolbar, just like you would to center text with Microsoft Word.

▶ Have fun customizing the templates, and don't be afraid to experiment! Keep in mind that since you're working with the template files on your computer's hard drive, no matter what you do, you can't irreparably screw up the template. There will always be a pristine copy of the website's template files on the book's CD that you can recopy to your computer should the need arise.

With that, it's time to get started examining how to use Composer to customize the family/personal website template!

Changing the Upper-Left Image

Each page in the family/personal website contains an image in the upper-left corner of my dog, Sam. You are invited to add your own image here, such as a picture of yourself, your family, or your family's pet. To replace the picture of Sam with a picture of your own, you'll need to have the picture on your computer's hard drive. In the "Customizing the Family Pictures Page" section you'll learn how to get pictures of yourself or family onto your computer, so that you can add them to your website's pages.

To customize the upper-left image, first copy the image you want to replace it with into the same folder that you copied the website template files to. Next, launch Composer if you have not already done so. (Recall that this involves starting the Mozilla Browser, and then going to the Window menu and choosing the Composer option.) Next, open the template's homepage file, index.html, in Composer. This is accomplished by either clicking the Open icon in the Toolbar or by going to the File menu and selecting the Open File menu option.

Once you have opened the index.html page in composer, your screen should look similar to Figure 3.2.

To change the image of Sam to an image of your own, you'll need to open the Image Properties dialog box for the image. This can be done in one of a number of ways: by right-clicking on the image and selecting the Image Properties menu option; by double-clicking the image; or by single-clicking the image and then clicking on the Image icon in the Toolbar. Using any of these approaches will display the Image Properties dialog box (see Figure 3.3), from which you can customize the information about the displayed image.

The next section, "Specifying Image Properties," steps through the four tabs in the Image Properties dialog box and discusses how to replace the image of Sam with an image of your own. Keep in mind that you'll need to replace the image of Sam with your own image for each web page in the family/personal website template.

Specifying Image Properties

The Image Properties dialog box contains four tabs: Location, Dimensions, Appearance, and Link. These tabs contain settings to customize the selected image's properties. Let's look at each of these tabs one at a time.

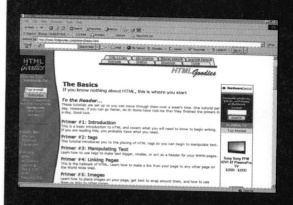

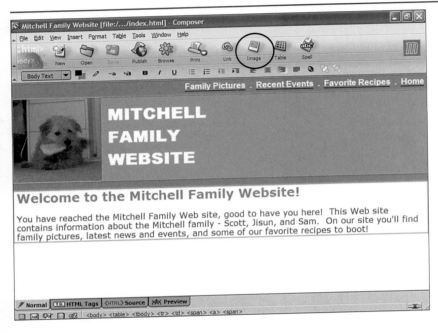

FIGURE 3.2
The index.html file has
been opened with
Composer.

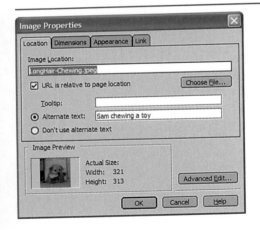

FIGURE 3.3
Customize the image from the Image Properties
dialog box.

The Location Tab

The Location tab, shown in Figure 3.3, allows
you to specify the file to display. To change the
upper-left image from one of my dog to one of
your own, click on the Choose File button and
select the image you want to display. Upon
doing so, a small preview of the image selected
will appear in the lower left corner of the
Image Properties dialog box.

Next, from the Location tab, you can set the Alternate text for the image. This is the text that is displayed in the image's place for those visitors who are using text-only browsers or who have configured their browsers to not display images. Realistically, very few web surfers fall into this category, so feel free to simply not provide any alternate text. If you decide not to provide alternate text, be sure to select the Don't use alternate text radio button.

The Dimensions Tab

The next tab, Dimensions, allows you to customize the width and height of the image. As Figure 3.4 shows, the Dimensions tab has

two radio buttons: Actual Size and Custom Size. If you leave Actual Size selected, the image will be displayed in its actual size. If you click Custom Size, you can specify the image size in either pixels or as a percentage of the browser's window.

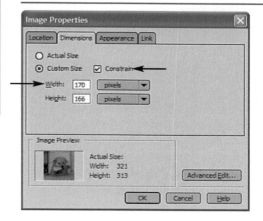

FIGURE 3.4

The image's size can be configured in the Dimensions tab.

The picture of Sam is scaled to a width of 170 pixels and a height of 166 pixels. As shown in the Image Preview section at the bottom of the dialog box in Figure 3.4, the actual image size is 321 pixels by 313 pixels.

Oftentimes an image will be resized so that it fits nicely on a page. The full-sized image of Sam is too large to fit nicely in the web page, hence it is scaled down to 170 by 166. When scaling images yourself, make sure to check the Constrain check box. This check box, if checked, makes sure that the ratio between the resized width and height remains the same as the original image's width and height ratio. By

THE SECRETS OF COLOR COMBINATIONS

Adam Polselli, the creator of this site, is very talented. We chose this site because he reveals how he chooses color combinations, but it's just a great site in general. Browse around and you'll find all kinds of goodies, including good writing, beautiful photographs, and some links to the tools he uses to create such a wonderful site.

His color scheme page shows you how he takes photos and picks colors from them to create color combinations that work for his Web page. So we tried it ourselves and it worked! Here's how to do it.

1. Open any simple paint program on your computer; it doesn't have to be Adobe Photoshop or anything expensive. We used the paint program that comes with the Microsoft operating system.

2. Open a photo that you find attractive.

3. Use the "pick color" tool that looks like an eye-dropper and click on a particular shade in the photo that you like

4. You'll see that the color you "picked" is available in your paint palette in your toolbox now.

It's that simple. Let nature choose your color scheme.

leaving this check box checked you ensure that resizing your image won't result in an image that is squished too fat or too thin.

When adding your own image, scale it so that it is at least 166 high. The family/personal website was designed to display an image precisely 166 pixels high. If you make the image shorter than 166 pixels, there will be whitespace beneath the image. When adding your own image, I would recommend that you

1. Select the Custom Size radio button.

2. Check the Constrain check box.

3. Enter 166 as the height.

NOTE

Realize that sizing the image smaller than its original size in the Dimensions tab only specifies to the browser to display the image as a certain size. Specifying a smaller size than the original does *not* reduce the image's file size. If you want to make the image a smaller file size, you need to use the resizing techniques discussed in the section "Resizing Digital Images," which can be found in the Bonus Materials chapter available on the book's accompanying CD.

The Appearances Tab

The Appearances tab (shown in Figure 3.5) allows you to configure how the image will appear within text. The Spacing section lets you specify how much spacing should appear between the left and right and top and bottom of the image and the text around the image. The Solid Border text box permits you to specify whether the image should have a border and, if so, how many pixels wide it should be.

Additionally, you can choose how to have the text aligned with the image. You can have the following text appear at the bottom of the image, the center, or the top. Alternatively, you can have the image flow within the text on the left or right.

For the family/personal website, I'd recommend not changing the values in the Appearances tab, as the template was designed to have no spacing around the image.

FIGURE 3.6

Use the Link tab to link the image to a URL.

FIGURE 3.5

The Appearances tab specifies how the text and image coexist.

The Link Tab

The final tab, the Link tab, allows you to specify a hyperlink for the image. That is, you can indicate that when the image is clicked, the user be whisked to a particular URL. A screenshot of the Link tab is shown in Figure 3.6.

Table 3.1: A Summary of the Image Properties Dialog Box's Tabs	
Tab	Description
Location	Choose the image to display from the Location tab. You can provide a Tooltip, which will be displayed when a visitor hovers her mouse over the image. Also, the Location tab allows you to specify an Alternate text, which is displayed in place of the image for those visitors whose browsers don't support images.
Dimensions	From the Dimensions tab you can indicate a custom height and width for the image.
Appearance	The Appearance tab allows you to indicate the top, bottom, left, and right spacing around the image (if any), along with how text flows around the image.
Link	You can configure your image so that when a visitor clicks it he is whisked to a different web page. If you want to enable this behavior, specify the URL to send the user in the Link tab.

Removing the Image Altogether

While some readers will like having a picture shown on each page, others might not want a picture shown at all. Fortunately, Composer makes it a cinch to remove the image from the upper-left corner. To strike the image from the web page altogether, simply right-click on the image and choose the Delete menu option.

Changing the Font

The text in the web page templates is displayed using a Verdana font. You can easily change the font for any text in Composer with the following steps:

1. Select the text whose font you want to change. The easiest way to do this is to place the mouse at the beginning of the text you want to select, and, holding down the mouse button, drag the mouse cursor until the text you want to modify is completely selected.

2. With the text selected, go to the Format menu. Choose the Font menu option and then pick a font from the list.

You can also change other text properties—such as the text color and style—through the Format menu. For example, imagine that you wanted to change the foreground color of the header text for a web page. (The header text in the homepage is "Welcome to the Mitchell Family Website!" and is displayed in a turquoise color.) To change this text's foreground color to, say, red, you'd first select the text and then go to the Format menu and choose the Text Color menu option. This will display the Text Color dialog box (see Figure 3.7), from which you can select a new foreground color.

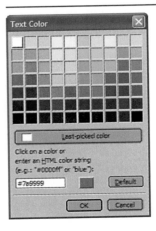

FIGURE 3.7
Pick the text's foreground color from the Text Color dialog box.

To make the font bold, italic, or underlined, first select the text and then go to the Format menu's Text Style menu. From there you can see the various formatting options.

> **TIP**
> To make the selected text bold, underline, or italic, you can also click on the appropriate B, I, or U icons in the Toolbar.

Adding and Removing Pages from the Template

The family/personal website template comes with four web pages: a homepage, a family pictures page, a recent events page, and a favorite recipes page. As we discussed earlier, though, you might very well want to add additional pages, or remove some of the pre-packaged pages.

CUSTOMIZING THE TEMPLATE

Removing a page from the site simply entails removing the links from the other web pages to the page you wish to snip from the site. For example, imagine that you didn't want to have a favorite recipes page on your family/personal website. To accomplish this, you'd need to open the homepage, family pictures page, and recent event page in Composer, and remove the link at the top to the Recent Events page. Removing the link is as simple as selecting the link text and hitting Delete.

NOTE

Keep in mind that you will need to remove *all* links to the page you want to remove. Be sure to open all other pages in Composer and remove any links you find pointing to the page to be removed.

To add a new page to the template, you need to create a new web page whose look and feel mimics that of the other pages in the template. Creating a new web page using the template can be done in one of two ways:

- ▶ By creating a new web page in Composer, and then copying and pasting the entire contents of a template page to the new page, or
- ▶ By going to the File menu and choosing the Save As menu option, which has the effect of saving an existing template web page with a different file name.

Once you have created the new web page and inherited the template's look and feel, you can customize the page's content as needed. For example, if you added an additional page that

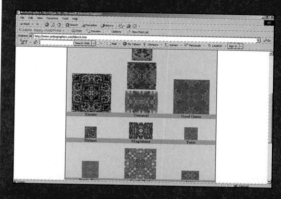

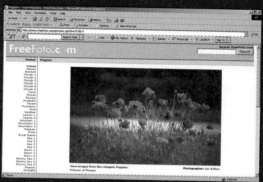

CAN'T BEAT FREE WEB GRAPHICS

Not artistic? Find free web graphics on the web to download for your own use. We found a site that categorizes free web graphics for you (http://www.freegraphics.com/). You can find buttons, bars, backgrounds, and clip art on many sites. Make sure to read the licensing information with each site. Sometimes the graphic images are only free if you're using them on a non-profit or personal basis. Here is a small list of cool sites we found:

Ambographics.com—offers lots of beautiful patterned backgrounds

Mikebonnell.com—has surreal-looking backgrounds and images

freefoto.com—where you can download stock quality photos for free listed important dates for your family, the content for this page would include the dates and their meanings (anniversaries, birthdays, graduations, and so on). After you have created the content for the new page, save the web page by going to the File menu and choosing the Save menu option.

Once you have created and saved the new page, the next step is to add a link from all other web pages in the site to the new page. As Figure 3.1 showed, each page has a list of links along the top. You'll need to add a link up top to the new page you created.

To add a link, start by clicking your mouse where you want the link to appear, perhaps between the Family Pictures and Recent Events links. Next, type in the text for the link, such as "Important Dates", followed by a period, which is used as a separator between each link.

The final step is to link the text you just entered to the new web page you created. To accomplish this, select the text you just added, go to the Insert menu, and choose the Link menu option. This will display the Link Properties dialog box, shown in Figure 3.8.

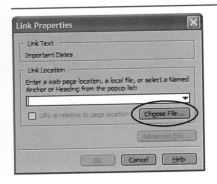

FIGURE 3.8
Select the page to link to using the Choose File button.

From the Link Properties dialog box, choose the file you want the user whisked to when they click the link. Since this link needs to take the user to the newly created page, click the Choose File button and select the page you added just a moment ago. Finally, click the OK button to create a hyperlink to the newly created page.

> **NOTE**
> Don't forget to add a link to the newly created page in all of the web pages in the site. If there are no links to the newly created page, then your visitors won't be able to get to the new page unless they manually enter the URL of the page in their browser's Address bar.

Customizing the Family Pictures Page

While family/personal websites are great for sharing recent events, recipes, and important dates, the main attraction to these types of websites is the family pictures. With digital cameras and scanners, it's incredibly easy to share pictures of your family, pets, vacations, and special events with friends and extended family.

"The family/personal website template contains a Family Pictures page from where you can share your family's photographs with others."

The family/personal website template contains a Family Pictures page from where you can share your family's photographs with others. In order to get started posting your pictures online, you will need to have the pictures you want to share in a digital format. If you own a digital camera, the photos stored on the camera are already in the needed format. If you want to put film pictures online, you have a couple options. If the picture already exists, you will need to get your hands on a *scanner*.

> **NOTE**
>
> A *scanner* is a piece of equipment that takes papers, pictures, or other flat documents, and makes a digital copy. Scanners are like copier machines, but rather than printing out a copy of the document being scanned, a scanner saves the image to a computer. Scanners are available at numerous stores like Best Buy, Circuit City, and so on, and can range in price from $50.00 to $500.00 dollars.

If you have taken pictures that you've yet to develop, you might be able to get the photographs developed as digital images. For an extra few bucks, you can get a CD of your pictures along with the developed photos.

> **NOTE**
>
> The book's CD includes a Bonus Materials chapter that has an in-depth discussion on digital images, including important digital imaging terminology and techniques for optimizing digital images.

Figure 3.9 shows a screenshot of the Family Pictures page, when viewed through Composer. Notice that the Family Pictures page contains a collage of pictures. Each image was added by going to the Insert menu and choosing the Image menu option. This will display the Image Properties dialog box, which we saw back in Figures 3.3 through 3.6. From the Image Properties dialog box, you can select the image you want to display and scale it accordingly. (All images shown on the Family Pictures page, for instance, were scaled so that they were no greater than 200 pixels wide or 200 pixels tall.)

In the next section you'll see how you can add your own images to the Family Pictures page. Before you add your own pictures, though, you'll likely want to take a minute to remove those pictures included with the template. To accomplish this, open the Family Pictures page in Composer and select the image(s) you want to delete. Delete the selected image(s) by hitting the Delete button, or by going to the Edit menu and choosing the Delete menu option.

Adding New Images

Adding a new image to the Family Pictures web page involves two steps:

1. Copy the images from your digital camera or scanner to the same folder where you copied the template web pages.

2. Insert the image into the page via the Insert menu's Image menu option.

IDEA GALLERY

http://www.andybudd.com/

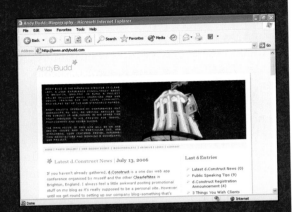

GREAT PERSONAL WEBSITE

It seems like everyone has a blog these days. Most of the searching we did for personal sites were actually weblogs created on sites such as Blogger.com, Tripod.com, BlogStudio.com, or a number of other hosting sites. Others, like this, were created with Movable Type. Blogs look like other web pages except that they work more like an online diary or journal. You can make entries as often as you like and visitors can leave comments if you allow them. We also chose this site because it has great information and links for you as beginning web developers. He recommends some good web design books and sends you to other sites that he thinks are cool or informative.

If you want to find out more about Movable Type, visit their website at http://www.movabletype.org/. They offer some great templates to use if you don't feel like designing your own columns and layout. You can also copy code for common things like RSS feeds, indexing features, comments listings.

Copying files from your digital camera or scanner differs on what brand of camera or scanner you have, so you'll have to refer to your camera or scanner's instructions to accomplish step 1. If you had your film developed into a CD, you'd just need to copy over the images from the CD to the appropriate folder.

Once the images have been copied over, open the Family Pictures page in Composer, if you haven't already. To insert an image, go to the Insert menu and select the Image menu option (or, optionally, click the Image icon in the Toolbar). This will display the Image Properties dialog box.

From the Locations tab (refer back to Figure 3.3), click the Choose File button and pick the image file you want to display. From the Dimensions tab (refer back to Figure 3.4), you can scale the image's height and width.

As Figure 3.9 shows, you can place images either side-by-side, or beneath one another. To place images side-by-side, simply insert one image right after the other. To create some space between the images, use the space bar to add space on the same line, or hit the Enter key to have the image appear on the following line. You can also add spacing around the top, bottom, left, and right of an image through the Appearance tab (refer back to Figure 3.5).

NOTE

Make sure that the image file you add exists in the same folder as the web page. You'll see why this is important in the "Publishing Your Family/Personal Website" section, but for now realize that it is vital to having the image display properly for users visiting your website.

FIGURE 3.9

The Family Pictures page, when viewed in Composer.

Publishing Your Family/Personal Website

At this point you have customized the web pages for the family/personal template, but these web pages still reside on your local computer, and are not accessible to others via the Internet. As discussed in Chapter 2, "Creating a Website," these files must be placed on a computer that has a dedicated connection to the Internet. Recall that there are a couple of steps you must go through to secure a public Internet website. Assuming you have completed these steps, publishing your Composer-created web pages is a breeze.

To publish a particular page, go to the File menu and choose Publish. This will display the Publish Page dialog box, which contains two tabs: Publish and Settings. As discussed in Chapter 2, the Settings tab allows you to specify information about the FTP server for the website as well as username and password information for the FTP server. You'll need to enter the FTP information provided by your web hosting provider in the Settings tab.

Once you have filled out the Settings tab, go to the Publish tab, which is shown in Figure 3.10. The Publish tab allows you to customize how the web page is published on the server. The default settings shown in Figure 3.10 are typically sufficient. To publish the web page, simply click the Publish button.

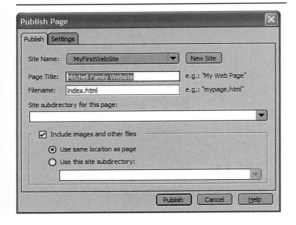

FIGURE 3.10

The Publish Page dialog box is used for publishing a web page to a public web server.

If the page is published successfully, you should see a dialog box like the one shown in Figure 3.11. This dialog box indicates the success or failure of publishing the web page and any associated files.

FIGURE 3.11

The index.html page has been published successfully!

Note that the dialog box in Figure 3.11 shows that two files have been uploaded to the web server—index.html and LongHair-Chewing.jpeg. What about the other web pages, such as pictures.html, events.html, and recipes.html? Those need to be uploaded too.

Unfortunately, with Composer you have to manually publish each of these files separately. That is, you need to open each file to publish in Composer, go to the File menu, and choose the Publish menu option.

NOTE

Notice that when you publish a file to the web server, any image files in the web page are automatically published as well. For example, when the homepage, index.html, is published, two files are uploaded to the web server: index.html and LongHair-Chewing.jpeg. **The** LongHair-Chewing.jpeg **is the image file of Sam that is in the upper-left corner of the homepage.**

Placing Linked Files in the Same Folder

Throughout this chapter when adding hyperlinks to other web pages or image files, I have stressed the important of placing the web pages or image files being linked to in the same folder as the page you are currently working on. If you do not do this, when a user visiting your site clicks on the link, they will not be taken to the desired page. Rather, they will see an error message informing them that the file requested could not be found.

Additionally, underneath the file name in the Link Properties dialog box there is an option called URL is relative to page location. When adding a link, this check box should be checked. After choosing a file by clicking the Choose File button, if the check box is unchecked, the text that appears in the drop-down list will look like file://*pathToTheFile/FileName*. If the check box is checked, the text in the drop-down list will have just the file name, and not the file://*pathToTheFile/* prepended.

It is important that the file://*pathToTheFile/* text does not appear before the file name. If it does,

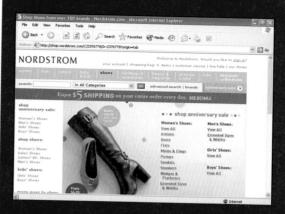

WHAT MAKES YOUR SITE STAND OUT FROM THE CROWD? WHY TO INVEST IN SEARCHING AND BROWSING

This site is a good one to review when you have lots of items or information to display. This major retailer has thousands of items that are organized under many categories. Those categories are then broken into subcategories, which provide easier site navigation. The items are often under more than one category, offering the user an efficient way to get to the same item. For instance, this site touts itself as the world's biggest shoe store. As you can imagine, that is a lot of shoes, and can be daunting when you are looking for something specific like loafers or boots. The intuitive organization offers categories such as Women's, Men's, Kids, and brands at the first level, but then Women's is broken down into 20 categories, ranging from flats to wedding shoes. More timesaving categories allow you to search by price, brand, bestseller, or "what's new." Of course, if you have the time, you can certainly click on "search all", and review every style, price, brand, and color! Providing the right categories is important when dealing with lots of items, as visitors can quickly they can find what they are looking for and will most likely result in additional visits to your site.

either uncheck the URL is relative to page location option, which will get rid of the offending text, or simply click on the text and delete the offending text manually.

You may be wondering why it is so important to have the URL is relative to page location check box checked. If you leave this unchecked, or leave in the file://pathToTheFile/ text, when the web page is published to the publicly available web server, these hyperlinks that were not successfully created will render as broken links in your visitor's web browsers.

> "Be sure to check the URL is relative to page location check box for each hyperlink you create, and your hyperlinks will work properly for all web visitors."

A broken link is a hyperlink that, when clicked, displays an error informing the user that the web page cannot be found. The reason this error occurs is because for links created without URL is relative to page location checked, the hyperlink's URL is published as file://pathToTheFile/FileName, which is the path and file name on your desktop computer. When a user clicks this link, their web browser will see the file:// and will attempt to locate a file on their computer's hard drive located in the specified path and with the specified file name. This file will likely not exist on their computer, and, hence, they will get an error message informing them the file could not be found.

What is important to realize is that since the file exists on your computer, if you are testing your website from your computer, these links will render fine because you have these files on your computer! However, others will not be

able to navigate through your website via these improperly created hyperlinks.

The short of it is, just be sure to check the URL is relative to page location check box for each hyperlink you create, and your hyperlinks will work properly for all web visitors.

Testing the Website

After you have published each web page for the family/personal website, take a moment to check out your website through a web browser. Launch your web browser and enter the URL to your website—in doing so you should see your family/personal website's homepage.

Click around on the hyperlinks and make sure all pages are accessible. If you get an error message when clicking on a hyperlink chances are the error is due to one of two causes:

First, the error might have occurred because you forgot to publish the web page that the hyperlink was pointing to. Remember that every web page that you created with Composer must be published to the public website. So make sure that the web page you are having trouble accessing was, indeed, published (and published successfully).

If you are certain that the web page you are requesting has indeed been published, then the error might be due to a broken link. That is, the hyperlink you clicked on is directing the user to a URL of a web page that does not exist. This could be due to having created a hyperlink to an existing file, but then later changing the file name and not updating the hyperlink's URL. Also, it might be due to not having checked the URL is relative to page location check box in the Link Properties dialog box. (See the "Placing Linked Files in the Same Folder" section earlier in this chapter for more details on this check box.)

In either case, you'll need to reopen the web page that contains the offending link, fix the link problem, and republish the page.

Summary

Customizing a website template with Composer can be both fun and easy. The family/personal website template presented in this chapter had a homepage and three sections: a series of digital photographs, the latest family news, and favorite family recipes. As you saw, customizing the existing pages—changing the text content, altering the colors, selecting a different font or formatting, and so on—are all very easy to accomplish with Composer. You can edit a web page just like you would edit a document with a word processor program.

In addition to working with the provided template web pages, you are encouraged to add additional pieces to your family/personal website so that the site is customized for you and your family. As discussed in this chapter, to add new pages you start by creating a new web page with the layout as another page in your template. From there, you can customize the new page's content. After this, all that remains is to update the other pages so that they provide a hyperlink to the newly created page.

In addition to customizing the template, we looked at how to publish the template to a web server once the customizations had been completed. To publish your web pages, you need to load each web page in Composer and choose the Publish menu option from the File menu. Publishing your web page will upload the actual web page along with any images displayed in the page. Once all of your web pages have been uploaded to the website, anyone with an Internet connection can view your site through a browser!

CHAPTER 4

Creating an Online Storefront

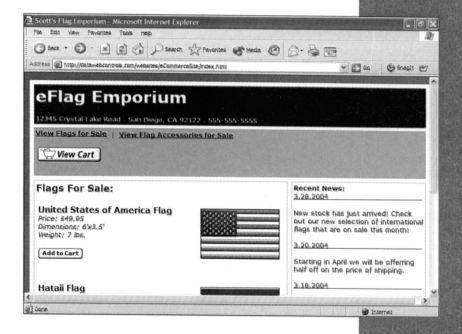

As the popularity of the Internet has ballooned over the years, many businesses have begun making their inventory available for purchase online. These types of websites marry commerce and the Internet, and are hence referred to as eCommerce websites. There is a plethora of eCommerce websites selling a wide range of products online. Amazon.com, one of the most well-known eCommerce sites, sells a vast array of products, from books to video games and DVDs to kitchenware and garden tools.

> *"As the popularity of the Internet has ballooned over the years, many businesses have begun making their inventory available for purchase online. These types of websites marry commerce and the Internet, and are hence referred to as eCommerce websites."*

Successful eCommerce websites have been built for both companies choosing to sell strictly online, and those companies who have had decades of history selling products in traditional brick and mortar stores. For example, Amazon.com is one of many companies that sell products exclusively on the Internet. That is, there are not any Amazon.com stores where you can stroll in and peruse the inventory.

Wal-Mart, the world's largest brick and mortar retailer with close to 5,000 stores worldwide, also has an eCommerce site— http://www.WalMart.com.

An eCommerce website must provide the following functionality:

- ▶ Display the items for sale along with their prices.
- ▶ Provide a means for a user to add one or more items to his "shopping cart."
- ▶ Accept payment information from a customer. (This typically involves the customer providing his credit card number.)

In this chapter you will build your very own eCommerce website that implements these features.

NOTE

The three requirements for an eCommerce site— listing the items for sale, providing a shopping cart, and accepting payment—are the minimum needed. Many eCommerce websites offer additional functionality, such as searching the products for sale, sorting the products by price or name, and allowing users to leave feedback about various products.

The eCommerce site we'll be creating this chapter will not include any of these more advanced features. The site will, however, be fully functional, allowing visitors to buy products directly from our website.

Accepting credit card payments and maintaining a shopping cart are anything but trivial tasks. Fortunately PayPal provides a Merchant Account program that provides a means for processing credit card payments and for supporting a shopping cart interface. There are no upfront costs associated with using the PayPal Merchant Account—the only cost is a small percentage of the total sales. The "Creating a PayPal Merchant Account" section discusses these fees and how to get started creating a PayPal Merchant Account.

Examining the eCommerce Website Template

All eCommerce websites provide a core set of functionality. Since the purpose of an eCommerce website is to provide a means for a visitor to purchase products online, the eCommerce site must list the products for sale, allow the user to add one or more products to his shopping cart, and finally provide a means for the user to purchase the products.

The eCommerce site template is one for a fictional company—eFlags Direct—that sells flags online. eFlags Direct sells both flags and flag accessories, such as flag poles, ropes, clips, and so on. The eFlags Direct template breaks up its products for sale into two categories: Flags and Flag Accessories. From the Flags category, users can add one or more flags to their shopping cart.

In addition to listing the products for sale, shoppers must be able to add products to their shopping cart. Creating a shopping cart is not a trivial task, and requires advanced computer programming skills that are far beyond the scope of this book. Fortunately, PayPal offers a shopping cart that can be plugged into the eCommerce website template by inserting a few lines of HTML.

The last vital piece of an eCommerce website is accepting payment, which involves showing the user their balance due. The amount they owe is typically the sum of the products purchased, any sales tax that needs to be added, plus any shipping costs. After reviewing their shopping cart and balance due, the user is prompted to enter their credit card information and complete the transaction.

As with the shopping cart, creating a web page to provide a bill, to accept payment information, and to properly bill it, is far beyond the scope of this book. As with the shopping cart, PayPal provides a means for payment that can be plugged into our eCommerce website.

The eCommerce website template is shown in Figure 4.1. Notice that it's composed of two pages: a list of the flags for sale and a list of the flag accessories for sale. Each item for sale includes a picture, a description, and an Add to Cart button. Clicking the Add to Cart button adds the item to the user's PayPal shopping cart. A user can check out by clicking the View Cart hyperlink.

WHAT IS AN ONLINE SHOPPING CART?

If you've ever purchased something online, you likely are familiar with online shopping carts. For those who have not yet purchased something online, though, an online shopping cart is similar in concept to a grocery store shopping cart—it simply serves as a receptacle into which you can place your items prior to purchasing.

The user experience of an online shopping cart goes as follows: A visitor browses through the eCommerce website, checking out the products for sale. If she finds a particular item she'd like to purchase, she clicks the Add Item to Cart button next to the item of interest. This adds the item to the shopping cart. At this point the shopper can continue to browse through the items for sale, adding additional items to the shopping cart.

Once our shopper has finished browsing and is ready to check out, she can click a Checkout button that will present her with a bill and ask for payment information. At this time our shopper would enter her credit card information.

Working with the eCommerce website template will require a little more customization than required with previous templates. First, you will have to create a free merchant account through PayPal.com. Then, based on your merchant information, you will need to tailor the Add to Cart button and View Cart hyperlink.

NOTE

In the next chapter, "Selling Products with an eBay Store," you'll see how to use eBay Stores to list your products for sale as well as process payment from customers. eBay Stores make getting started selling online easier, but limits the flexibility you have in customizing the online store front's appearance. Before deciding which approach to use—creating a custom online store front or using eBay Stores—I'd encourage you to read both this chapter and the next first, and then make an educated decision based upon your business's needs.

67

FIGURE 4.1
The eCommerce website template.

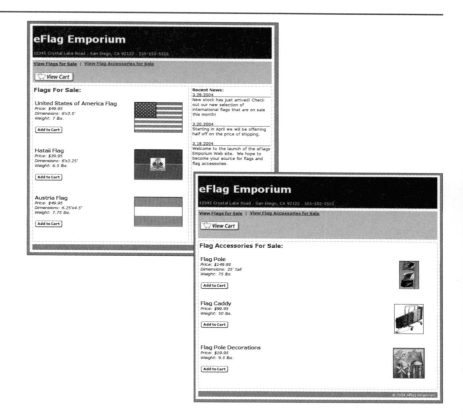

Customizing the Homepage

The eCommerce website template's homepage starts by listing the company's name, address, and contact information at the top of the page. Underneath that, there is a series of navigational hyperlinks listing the product categories, along with a View Cart button.

To change the name of one of the product categories, click on the product category text and, using the keyboard, alter the link's text. To change the URL to which the hyperlink points to, right-click on the link and choose the Link Properties menu option. This, as you've seen in

previous chapters, will display the Link Properties dialog box, from which you can change the link's location.

TIP

To create a new navigational link, set the focus to the point where you want the new link to be placed. Then, go to the Insert menu and choose the Link menu option. This will display the Link Properties dialog box, prompting you for the link's text and location.

The View Cart button links to PayPal.com's website and, when clicked, displays the items in the user's shopping cart and provides a checkout process. You'll need to configure this View Cart button based on your own PayPal.com merchant account. The next section examines the steps necessary to create a merchant account and to configure the View Cart button.

Underneath the navigation hyperlinks are two table cells. The one on the left lists the flags for sale. The one on the right lists recent site news.

The template contains descriptions and pictures for flags. If you're selling something other than flags, you'll of course need to change the description and pictures. To edit the picture, right-click on the picture and choose the Image Properties menu option. This will display the Image Properties dialog box from which you can specify the image file to use, along with its dimensions and other aesthetic properties.

At the end of each product description there's an Add to Cart button. This button ties into PayPal.com to integrate a shopping cart with the eCommerce site. To have this button work correctly, you'll need to first create a PayPal.com merchant account.

Configuring the Add to Cart Buttons

The next challenge is to allow visitors to add items from the View Flags for Sale and View Flag Accessories for Sale web pages to their shopping cart. In order to accomplish this, you can use PayPal's Merchant Account tools, which include capabilities to add a shopping cart to a website, as well as a means for processing credit card payments.

To allow visitors to add a flag or flag accessory to their shopping cart, add a button titled, Add to Cart for each item for sale. By clicking this button, the specified item will be added to the user's shopping cart. The shopper may then add additional items to their shopping cart and eventually pay for their purchased items.

Before you can examine what needs to be done to provide the Add to Cart button for each product, you first need to register for a PayPal Merchant Account. There are no costs or fees associated with creating a PayPal Merchant Account, so feel free to follow along in creating your own Merchant Account!

Creating a PayPal Merchant Account

PayPal—on the Web at http://www.paypal.com—was founded in 1998 to allow individuals and businesses to send and receive payments easily, reliably, and securely. Anyone can create a free PayPal account, and then transfer money into their account by sending PayPal a check, by having the money drafted from their bank, or through a credit card transaction. Once the money is in your account, you can send the money to another PayPal member by simply supplying that person's email address and the amount you want to send. You can, at any time, withdraw all or part of the funds in your PayPal account, either through a direct deposit into your bank account or via a check.

> **NOTE**
>
> In 2002, PayPal was acquired by eBay. Not surprisingly, eBay strongly encourages using PayPal as a means for paying for auctions on eBay.

Since its inception, PayPal has continued to offer more features to facilitate its main goal of allowing online payments. One added feature is the PayPal Merchant Account, which is designed to allow individuals and small businesses to accept payments online. The Merchant Account provides a shopping cart and a payment process, both of which reside on PayPal's website.

The Merchant Account works as follows:

1. A user visits your site and finds a product they are interested in buying.

2. The shopper clicks the Add to Cart button next to the desired product's name, which takes them to PayPal's website, adds the item to the shopping cart, and displays the shopping cart. The user can, at that point, check out by paying for the item, or can return to your website to continue shopping.

3. When the customer has completed their shopping, they return to the shopping cart on PayPal's website and enter their payment information. After successfully providing their payment information, they are sent back to your website.

If a customer makes a purchase from your website of, say, $10.00, what happens is the following: PayPal charges the user's credit card for $10.00. After the monies have been cleared,

IF YOU BUILD IT, THEY WILL COME (RIGHT?)

Marketing Find was the best site we found that tells you how to let people know about your website. There are so many ways to reach customers through the Internet—email newsletters and promotions, online ads, and paying for words on search engines such as Google. How do you know what's cost effective? How do you measure success? This site is like a mini Internet marketing class. Check out their article and recommended resources for analyzing your website traffic called "Yo! Analyze This!" Want to do email marketing, but don't know how to get your customer's attention? This site has an entire section devoted to email marketing and newsletters. Even the ads on this site are a great resource to you as beginning web developers. We found advertisers who will measure your site traffic for you; others who will create, send, and track your email campaigns; and companies who will drive targeted traffic to your website.

Check out the section of their site called "Marketing Math." They provide an online ROI calculator for you. Just plug some metrics on your advertising campaign and your revenue, and their calculator will tell you if you received a fair return for your investment.

PayPal takes a small percentage of the sale—2.2% plus a 30 cent transaction fee. The remainder of the balance is then credited into your PayPal account. Also, after a payment has been processed, you are sent an email informing you of the purchase so that you can ship the shopper's goods to her.

Figure 4.2 provides an illustration of the process of a visitor making a purchase from your website. What's important to realize is that the shopping cart and payment processing are done entirely on PayPal's website. This has several advantages, the two big ones being that you can sell products on your site without needing to process credit card transactions or concern yourself with the complexities involved in setting up an online shopping cart and payment processing.

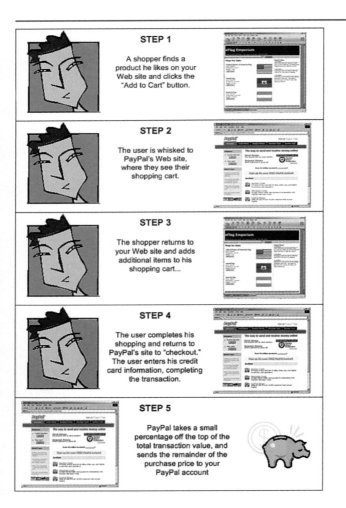

FIGURE 4.2

PayPal handles the shopping cart and payment processing on their website.

STEP 1

A shopper finds a product he likes on your Web site and clicks the "Add to Cart" button.

STEP 2

The user is whisked to PayPal's Web site, where they see their shopping cart.

STEP 3

The shopper returns to your Web site and adds additional items to his shopping cart...

STEP 4

The user completes his shopping and returns to PayPal's site to "checkout." The user enters his credit card information, completing the transaction.

STEP 5

PayPal takes a small percentage off the top of the total transaction value, and sends the remainder of the purchase price to your PayPal account

PayPal offers accounts for both individuals and businesses. Business accounts have access to the Merchant Account features by default. Personal accounts are broken into two classes:

- Basic Accounts
- Premier Accounts

Basic Accounts do not impose any sort of fee on receiving or sending money, but do not offer the features available with the Merchant Account. Upgrading to a Premier account grants you access to the Merchant Account tools, but beware—*all* payments—not just credit card payments—will be subject to a 2.2%–2.9% fee off the top.

If you have an existing PayPal basic personal account, the first step is to determine what type of account you have. To do this, log in to your PayPal account. In the Account Overview screen you will see what type of account your have. As Figure 4.3 shows, I have a U.S. Personal Account.

If you do not have a Premier account, you will need to upgrade your account. In the Account Overview screen you should find a link titled Upgrade Account. Click this to begin the upgrade process.

FIGURE 4.3

The Account Overview screen informs existing PayPal members what type of account they have.

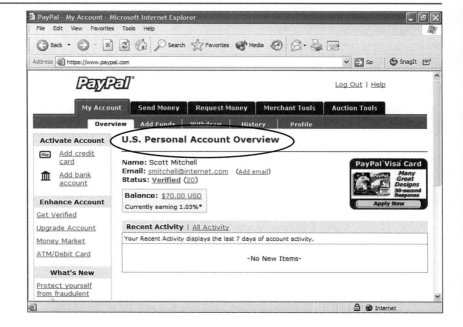

IDEA GALLERY

http://www.Westelm.com

THINK LIKE A CUSTOMER

West Elm is a contemporary home furnishing site that offers more than attractive home furniture. It offers the user a shopping experience similar to one they would have at an actual store with one advantage—users can go directly to the item they are interested in purchasing without going through the entire store. The site is organized by item, such as sofas, accessories, and so on, or you can shop by room, such as living room, office, and so forth. It is quite simple in its design, offering a clean, clear way to shop for home furnishings. Selected items can be displayed in a larger format or in your chosen color, taking the guesswork out when looking only at a color swatch. The site is very usable, which is important to keep in mind when designing a site. Simply, the easier navigation is, the cleaner your design makes a better experience for your visitor. Making things complex when they don't need to be only frustrates your visitor. And most often the goal is repeat visitors, so providing a pleasant experience at first click is an important goal for any website designer.

If you do not have a PayPal account at all, you will need to create a new Premier account. This process is free, and only takes a few moments of your time. Start by going to PayPal's homepage—http://www.paypal.com—and click on one of the Sign Up links shown in Figure 4.4.

You will first be asked whether you want to create a Personal or Business account, and for which country (see Figure 4.5). If you choose a Personal account you will be asked for information such as your name, address, phone number, email address, and so on. If you create a business account, you will need to provide this information as well as information about the business, such as what field it's in, your role in the business, the business's official contact information, and so on.

If you opted to create a business account, you will be prompted for information about the business. After entering this information, you will be asked to provide the personal information shown in Figure 4.4. (If you created a personal account you will be taken directly to the screen shown in Figure 4.4.) Here you are asked to provide your name, address, phone number, email address, a password, and other information. For personal accounts, you can choose whether you want to create this account as a Premier account—choose Yes.

The final step involves sending a confirmation email to the email address you supplied. Follow the instructions in the email you receive to complete the registration process.

Congratulations! At this point you have created a PayPal account that has access to the Merchant Account features.

FIGURE 4.4
FIGURE 4.4

Click on one of the Sign Up links to create a new PayPal account.

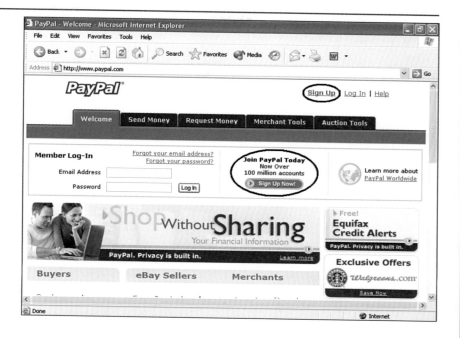

FIGURE 4.5

Choose to create a business or personal account.

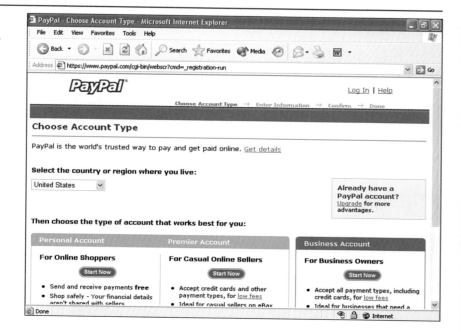

FIGURE 4.6
Provide your personal information.

Getting the Add to Cart Button HTML

In order to allow your visitors to add an item to their shopping cart, you need to add an Add to Cart button next to each product for sale on your website. The button, when clicked, will direct the user to PayPal's website, adding the item to the user's shopping cart.

> **NOTE**
>
> In the template, there already is an Add to Cart button. To customize the template for your site, you'll need to delete this button and add in your customized button.

"PayPal offers a wizard that steps you through the process of adding an Add to Cart button."

In previous chapters you saw how hyperlinks can be used to transfer a user from one web page to another. In addition to hyperlinks, there are also more involved techniques for transferring a user from one page to another. One such technique involves the use of *forms*. A thorough discussion of forms is beyond the scope of this book—it is mentioned solely because this is the technique used to transfer the user from our website to PayPal's website when adding an item to the shopping cart or when checking out.

Don't worry, you don't have to be a wiz at forms to create the Add to Cart buttons. Rather, PayPal offers a wizard that steps you through the process of adding an Add to Cart button. At the end of the wizard, you are given a snippet of HTML markup, which can be directly pasted into our web page where we want the Add to Cart button to appear.

The first step to generating the Add to Cart button HTML is to go to PayPal's website and log in. Next, click on the Merchant Tools tab at the top of any PayPal web page. This will take you to the Merchant Account homepage, shown in Figure 4.7. From the Merchant Account homepage, click the Paypal Shopping Cart hyperlink.

This will begin a two-page process where you will be asked a number of questions about the product being sold, such as its title, price, item number, and other information. Let's create the button HTML for the United States of America flag. The first page of the two-page wizard starts by asking you to supply the Item Name, Item ID, Price of Item, and Currency.

TIP

The Item ID field is optional, but is useful if you are selling a large number of items. When a user makes a purchase from your site, you'll receive an email with a list of what products she bought. This will include the product name, along with the Item ID (if provided). So, if you keep track of your products by some ID, enter this ID into the Item ID field.

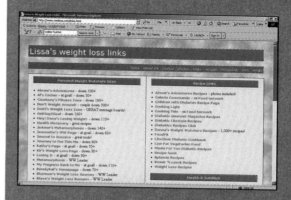

SIMPLE IS GOOD

What's so great about Lissa's Weight Loss page? It's simple. We love this site because it has everything you'd ever want to find about one thing—weight loss. The first page is a jumping off place for just about everything you might need—other people's personal weight loss sites, recipe links, health and nutrition links, fitness and exercise, newsgroups, and weight loss calculators. Each category has a bulleted list of links. That's it.

We've seen other sites that offer plenty of information, but why bother visiting when the pages are so complicated and busy that you can't find what you want? You've seen those kinds of sites—different font sizes all over the place, pictures everywhere, flashing images, and an obnoxious array of colors.

So what's the lesson? Your site doesn't have to be fancy or beautiful to be great. Fill it with content that people want and make it easy for them to find things—that's it.

FIGURE 4.7

From the Merchant Account homepage, click on the Paypal Shopping Cart link.

Figure 4.8 shows a screenshot of the first page of the wizard after suitable values have been entered into these fields for the United States flag. (Note that I arbitrarily chose 311 as the Item ID for the U.S. flag.)

After you have entered the product's name, ID, price, and so on, scroll down to the bottom of this first page. You'll be prompted to select an Add to Cart button. PayPal provides a default button (shown in Figure 4.9), but if you have a custom-made button you can supply the URL of this button image. I am going to opt to stick with the PayPal-provided image.

If you do not need to add any additional features, such as sales tax or shipping costs,

you can click the Create Button Now button. Otherwise, if you want to specify more advanced features, click the Add More Options button.

> **NOTE**
>
> If you clicked the Create Button Now because you did not need to specify shipping costs or sales tax information, feel free to skip over the "Specifying Sales Tax and Shipping Costs" section and go directly to the "Viewing the Button's HTML" section.

FIGURE 4.8

The first step involves providing information about the product for sale.

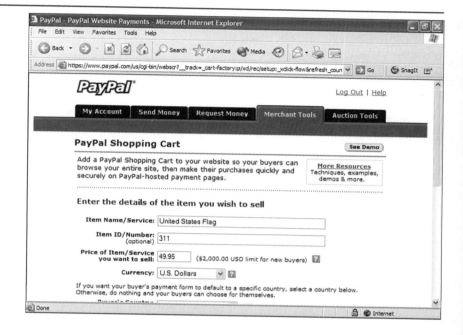

FIGURE 4.9

Click the Add More Options button to provide information on sales tax and shipping costs.

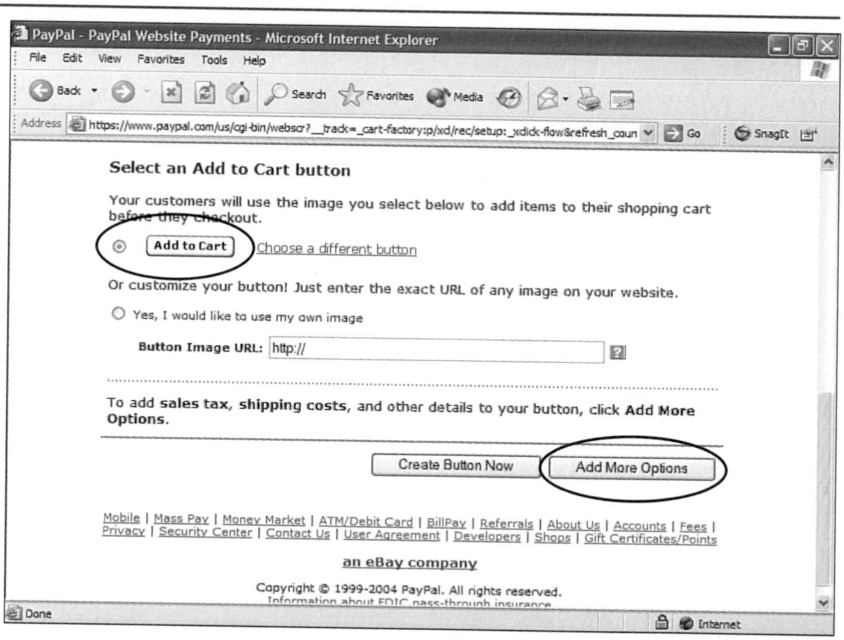

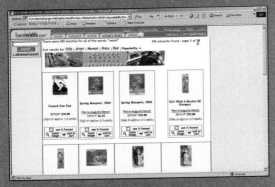

THE ART OF NAVIGATION

Shopping on the web is easy if the site you're visiting offers different ways to browse their products. Barewalls.com lets you find their artwork in a variety of ways—by style, by subject, by artist. They also categorize artwork into museum art, contemporary art, pop culture, and photography. Once you click on a category, you can sort your choices by popularity, size, price, and so on. This site knows how to exploit its advantages over brick and mortar art galleries and other art websites that don't offer such a variety of ways to find artwork.

If you're planning an ecommerce website, think about ways that customers will want to search your site. Make it as easy as possible for them to find the right products.

Specifying Sales Tax and Shipping Costs

If you click the Add More Options button from the first page of the wizard, you will be taken to the second page, where you can, among other things, specify sales tax and shipping cost. Figure 4.10 shows the Shipping and Sales Tax section on the second page. Note that by default there are no shipping costs or sales tax applied.

To provide a shipping cost, click the Edit button to the right of the shipping cost list. There are two types of shipping cost models that you can choose from:

▶ Flat—Here, the shipping cost is a flat cost based on price ranges. That is, you can opt to have all items between $0.00 and $9.99 cost, say, $2.50 to ship, while other items between $10.00 and $49.99 might cost $4.95 to ship.

▶ Percentage—Here, the shipping cost is a percentage of the total cost. You can enter different percentages for different price ranges. That is, you can have items between $0.00 and $100.00 require a shipping cost of 10% of the purchase price, while items above $100.00 could have a shipping cost of 7.5%.

To edit the sales tax, click the Edit button to the right of the Sales Tax Calculation section. The sales tax section lets you add certain taxes for shoppers from particular countries or U.S. states. For example, if your business is based in California, only California residents who purchase goods through your website need pay sales tax. PayPal allows you to specify what countries or states must pay sales tax and what the tax rate is for each state or country.

FIGURE 4.10
You can specify the shipping costs and sales tax.

When checking out, the customer's bill totals the sum of the prices of items purchased, plus the shipping costs, if specified, plus any sales tax, if specified and if applicable based on the buyer's residence.

There are some additional options on this web page, but these are a bit beyond the scope of this book. After providing the shipping and sales tax information, scroll down to the bottom of the page and click the Create Button Now button to view the button's generated HTML markup.

NOTE

You only need to set up the shipping costs and sales tax once. After specifying this information, it is stored on PayPal's web servers so that for all products you sell the sales tax and shipping cost information is applied.

Viewing the Button's HTML

After you have clicked the Create Button Now button—either in the first page of the wizard or after entering shipping and sales tax information—you will be taken to the final page that contains the HTML markup for the Add to Cart buttons. Figure 4.11 shows a screenshot of this page.

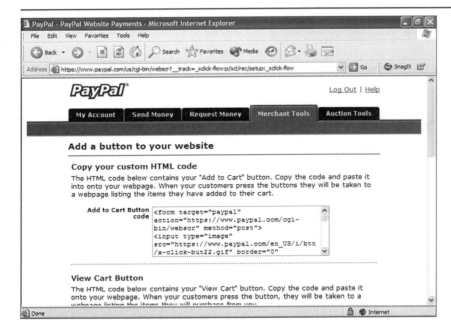

FIGURE 4.11
The HTML markup for the button has been generated.

There are actually two snippets of HTML on this page. The first one is in the textbox labeled "Add to Cart Button code." This HTML markup is what you will place next to the United States Flag product. Doing so will display an Add to Cart button. The second snippet of HTML is in the text box labeled "View Cart Button code."

The HTML in this second text box will be used to take the user to his shopping cart. Specifically, it will display a button titled View Cart. In the "Viewing the Shopping Cart" section you'll see how to add this View Cart button.

TIP

At the bottom of this page you'll find a button titled Create Another Button. Clicking this button will take you back to the first page of the wizard with your previous values pre-entered into the various text boxes. You'll need to create an Add to Cart button for each product for sale on our site. The Create Another Button button is a quick way to jump back and start creating a new button!

Adding the Add to Cart Button into the Template

To customize the template's Add to Cart button with your own PayPal.com merchant information, you'll need to first delete the existing Add to Cart button. Notice that around the button is a green, dashed border. To remove the Add to Cart button, right-click on this border and choose the Delete menu option.

NOTE

After deleting the Add to Cart button, the green, dashed border should disappear. If you still see the green, dashed border, but without the button, try again, making sure to right-click on the dashed border.

Once you have deleted the Add to Cart button in the template, you're ready to add your custom Add to Cart button. To accomplish this you'll need to copy and paste the HTML from the PayPal.com wizard's "Add to Cart Button code" text box to the appropriate location in the web page.

First go to the PayPal web page and copy the HTML in the first text box to your computer's clipboard. (This is accomplished by first selecting the text in the text box and then going to the Edit menu and choosing Copy.)

Now, return to the Composer window. To insert the HTML copied from the PayPal web page, go to the Insert menu and choose the HTML menu option. This will display the Insert HTML dialog box (shown in Figure 4.12). Paste the HTML from your computer's clipboard into this dialog box by hitting the Control (Ctrl) and V keys on your keyboard simultaneously.

After you have pasted in the HTML from the PayPal web page, click the Insert button to paste this HTML content into the web page.

IDEA GALLERY

http://www.thaigems.com

A GOOD PICTURE IS WORTH A THOUSAND WORDS

This site's pictures are great. Not only do they sell very tiny objects (gemstones), but their pictures are large enough and clear enough to view even the smallest details and cuts of each stone. If you want to sell products through your website or through a site like eBay, get a good digital camera and practice uploading photos to make sure they're attractive, but still small enough to load quickly for the viewer. If your page doesn't load within 30 seconds, visitors will probably leave.

JPEG is a good format for the Web because it compresses images so that they can load faster. Some photo programs such as Adobe's Photoshop Elements have the capabilities to help you save pictures for the Web. They give you choices in a dialog box and they handle the rest—the right compression, image sizing, and color features to make your pictures look great on your site. If you're going to edit photos yourself, here are a few guidelines. Most product pictures on websites are no larger than 400 x 400 pixels. Thaigems's largest pictures are about 200 x 200. The size of the file is important, too. Aim for 50KB or smaller.

FIGURE 4.12

The Insert HTML dialog box allows you to add HTML markup to a specific section of the web page.

Congratulations, you have added your first Add to Cart button! Now, this process needs to be repeated for each of the other products for sale. That is, you'll need to return to the PayPal website and repeat the wizard, entering in a different product's title, price, and other pertinent information. Do this for both the flag and flag accessories for sale.

NOTE

Realize that you only need to supply shipping costs and sales tax *once*. That is, you do not need to repeatedly provide this information for each button created.

Viewing the Shopping Cart

The final step in creating the eCommerce site is to add a View Cart button to the navigational bar at the top of each web page in the site

template. Recall that when generating the HTML markup for an individual Add to Cart button in the PayPal.com wizard, there were two text boxes of HTML—the first one contained the HTML markup for the Add to Cart button, while the second text box contained the HTML markup for the View Shopping Cart button. (Refer back to Figure 4.11 for a screenshot.) You need to paste the HTML from the second text box where you want the View Shopping Cart button to appear.

> *"The final step in creating the eCommerce site is to add a View Cart button to the navigational bar at the top of each web page in the site template."*

Like with the Add to Cart button, to accomplish this you'll first need to delete the View Cart button from each template page. Following that, you'll need to paste in the HTML from the wizard using the Insert menu's HTML option.

Once you have added your customized View Cart button, users will be able to view their cart's contents at any time by clicking on the View Cart button.

Tying It All Together—A True Online Shopping Experience

At this point you have created the essential pieces of an eCommerce site: You have listed the products for sale; each product has an Add to Cart button next to it, which adds it to the shopping cart; customers can provide their credit card information and purchase the goods in their shopping cart. Your task was made infinitely easier thanks to the Merchant Account tools provided by PayPal.

You're now ready to go live with your site! As discussed in the three previous chapters, this involves publishing each page. Take a moment to open each template's two web pages and publish them by clicking the Publish icon in the toolbar, or by going to File menu and selecting the Publish menu item.

Now that you've published your site, let's take a moment to look at the shopper's experience—from browsing the products, to adding items to the shopping cart, to paying for an order.

Figure 4.13 shows the "View Flags for Sale" web page. Note that each flag for sale has an Add to Cart button. If a visitor clicks, say, the Austrian Flag Add to Cart button, a new browser window opens showing the user their shopping cart (see Figure 4.14).

FIGURE 4.13

A shopper would first visit the "View Flags for Sale" web page.

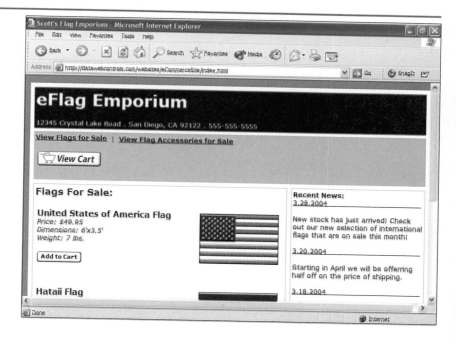

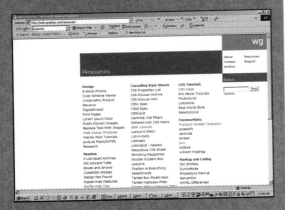

WEB RESOURCES GALORE

We thought this was a great resource site for those of you getting into web design and development. The links are divided into categories such as CSS (cascading style sheet) tutorials, design and web graphics, markup resources, and places to find stock photos and illustrations. This is a page that you can bookmark and visit whenever you need something for your site or when you're ready to learn some new trick. In the miscellaneous section, there's even a link to some nice little demos on Javascript flexible floats, image captions, titles, and CSS drop shadows.

What if you want to know how other people are setting up their web pages for the best user experience? Click on the link for web design practices, and you'll find help with navigation, e-commerce functions, and page layout. There are people whose only job is to analyze the usability of websites. Why not take advantage of this free advice?

As Figure 4.14 shows, the shopping cart lists the current items the user has added to their cart. From this page the user can update the quantity of items in their cart or remove items. By clicking the Continue Shopping button, the user will be returned to the "View Flags for Sale" web page, where they can add additional flags to their shopping cart. Figure 4.15 shows the shopping cart after the user returns to the "View Flags for Sale" web page and clicks the Add to Cart button for the United States Flag.

The user completes her purchase by clicking the Checkout button in the shopping cart. Doing so takes the shopper to a page that spells out the payment details and offers the user the opportunity to pay through an existing PayPal account (if they have one), or via a credit card. Figure 4.16 shows the first screen of the Payment Details page.

After progressing through the payment screens, which involves either logging in to an existing PayPal account or providing credit card information, the user is billed and your PayPal account is credited with the amount of the transaction less the percentage PayPal takes off the top.

After the transaction has completed, you will receive an email indicating what items the user has purchased and their shipping address. It is then your responsibility to send them their purchased goods in a timely manner.

FIGURE 4.14

Clicking the Add to Cart button takes the user to their shopping cart.

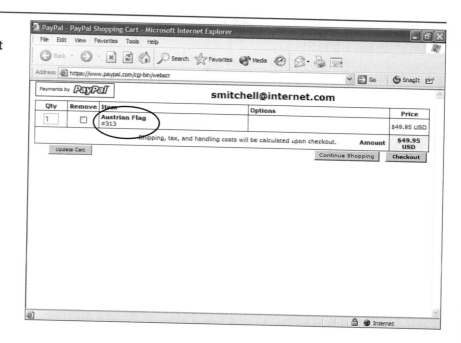

FIGURE 4.15

The user has added the United States Flag to her shopping cart.

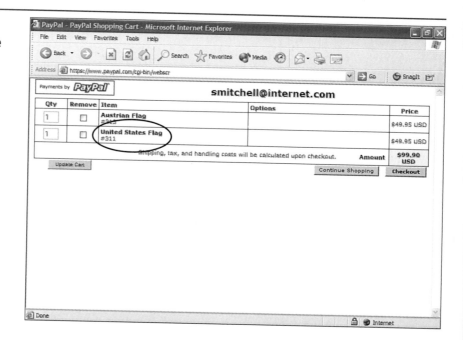

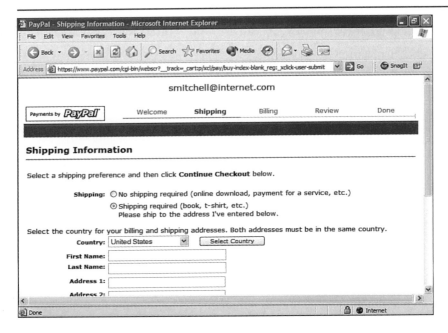

FIGURE 4.16

The user can pay for her purchase via an existing PayPal account or with a credit card.

Summary

In this chapter you learned how to create a fully functioning online store with the aid of PayPal's Merchant Account tools. All the complicated work of creating and maintaining a shopping cart, and processing credit card payments, is handled by PayPal for a small commission on sales.

The eCommerce site we built was a relatively simple one, containing just the bare features required: a listing of the products; an Add to Cart button for each product that, when clicked, added the item to the shopping cart; and a means for customers to check out and pay for their order. More advanced eCommerce sites typically contain additional features, such as customization features, search capabilities,

and customer feedback. Unfortunately, adding these sorts of features would require more advanced technologies than HTML, and therefore fall outside the scope of this book. Don't let the simplicity of the eCommerce website we created, though, take away from what we accomplished. In the span of one chapter we went from nothing to a website that provides a fully functioning online store front.

CHAPTER 5

Selling Products with an eBay Store

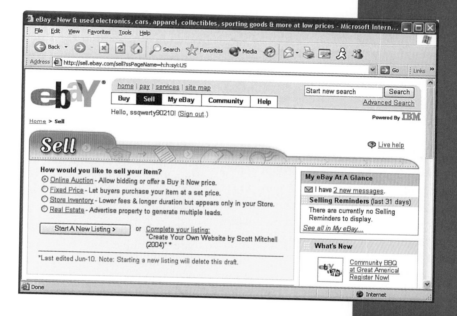

Over the past several years online shopping has evolved from a novelty to a standard means of business. A vast number of traditional, brick and mortar stores have an online presence, and an incalculable number of businesses operate solely on the Web, forgoing any sort of physical store presence. A June 2, 2005, article by Shihoko Goto for United Press International expresses the importance of online commerce in today's economy: "Online shopping is 'here to stay, no matter what sector,' said Dan Freeman, an assistant professor at the business department of the University of Delaware. 'There's really no particular product' that would not be a good item to buy online these days...."

As you learned in Chapter 4, "Creating an Online Storefront," selling items online is possible even if you're not a computer expert. The main challenges of selling online are having an online shopping cart that customers can fill with your products and providing a means to collect payment. In Chapter 4, you saw how to integrate PayPal's services within your own website to achieve these two aims.

The techniques discussed in Chapter 4 require that you create your own website from the ground up. This has its advantages—you can highly customize the look and feel of your online store—but it also carries with it a bit of legwork to start selling online. For starters, you have to create pages for each of your items for sale and, after an item sells, you have to manually remove it from your website's pages. And although the online storefront from the Chapter 4 is completely functional, it lacks features that entrepreneurs selling many items

online want, such as being able to easily add, edit, and remove the items for sale; view reports breaking down sales numbers; and so on. If you are selling only a few items online, the website created in Chapter 4 will likely fit your needs, but if you want to move hundreds of items each month, you'll quickly find that the custom online storefront from Chapter 4 does not scale.

> ## "Over the past several years online shopping has evolved from a novelty to a standard means of business."

This chapter looks at an alternative to creating a custom online storefront. Rather than building the web pages for the website yourself, you can use eBay Stores, a web application offered by eBay for individuals or businesses interested in a professional online storefront that can be set up easily and quickly. Since its creation in 1995, eBay has grown from a small auction site originally designed to sell Pez dispensers to a publicly traded multibillion dollar venture that hosts millions of auctions from around the world each and every day.

With its millions of ongoing auctions, it's no surprise that eBay has the infrastructure to handle order processing. With an eBay Store you are essentially paying to utilize this infrastructure, which includes a web-based interface to add items to your store, a search engine for your store, and order processing. For this service eBay charges a monthly fee, a minimal insertion fee for each item for sale, and a percentage of the final sales price.

NOTE

When deciding whether to use a custom online storefront website or an eBay Store, consider your business's anticipated needs. If you expect that you'll have dozens of unique items in inventory or will be selling hundreds of items or more per month, you should use an eBay Store. If, however, you are only selling a small number of unique items or expect to sell only a handful of items per month, the custom online storefront is a more attractive option, in part because eBay Stores imposes a monthly fee and in part because such a site affords greater customization in the site's appearance and layout.

Simplify the Sales Process with eBay Stores

There are many facets to running a successful online store. The most vital aspects, of course, are those directly tied to actually selling your product, which includes listing the items for sale, providing an easy user experience for online shoppers to purchase one or more items, and collecting and processing customers' payment information.

In addition to these vital aspects, successful online businesses also excel in other areas. Marketing is an important aspect for any business, online or not. After all, a customer must know that your store and products exist before she can buy them! Also important in any business is being able to analyze customer trends. If you run an online discount bookstore and find that customers are buying the *New York Times* bestseller books in droves while the self-help books remain unsold, you can use that information to increase your inventory of

bestsellers and think of new ways to market your slow-moving self-help books.

In Chapter 4, you examined only how to achieve the vital facets of building an online business. Specifically, you saw how to list the inventory for sale by extending the online storefront web page templates included on the book's CD and how to integrate PayPal to handle the online shopping cart and payment processing. Such a bare bones website makes considering marketing and business analysis features impractical. And you'll likely find that marketing is one of the most difficult challenges with any online venture—how do you attract visitors to your website?

If you are planning on selling dozens of items from your online store or are especially concerned about the marketing and business analysis aspects of your online business, you'll find eBay Stores to be superior to a custom online storefront website for selling merchandise online. With an eBay Store, you can list and remove items for sale through eBay's user-friendly web interface. eBay Stores also provides an assortment of marketing tools, including email lists, search engine keywords, and promotional flyers. eBay Stores also provides traffic and sales reports to better help you analyze sales patterns and trends.

Best of all, eBay Stores are hosted on eBay's website using eBay's familiar buying process. Customers who visit your store who are already familiar with eBay will feel at home when browsing your store or making purchases. Additionally, your eBay Store merchandise can, optionally, appear in the standard eBay auctions, meaning when visitors are searching eBay for a particular item, your store's inventory will show up in the results.

Before opening your eBay Store I highly encourage you to first become familiar with eBay, if you're not already. Create a free account, find a couple of items you are interested in buying, and make a bid. This will familiarize you with the process your customers will undergo when making a bid or buying one of your store's items.

Next, find some items around the house to sell and become comfortable with listing these items for auction. As you'll see later in this chapter the process for adding items to your online store is identical to listing items for auction.

The more comfortable you are with the eBay website and its user interface the more proficient a seller you'll be with your online store. This chapter does not provide an in-depth look into buying and selling items on eBay; rather, it focuses on establishing, customizing, and working with an eBay Store. If you are new to eBay and are concerned that you'll quickly become overwhelmed, don't worry. The eBay user experience is well-known for its ease of use, so don't be afraid to dive in head first. And if you do need some additional assistance, a number of great books are available that explain step-by-step how to buy and sell items on eBay. For those new to eBay I recommend Que Publishing's *Absolute Beginner's Guide to eBay*, by Michael Miller.

NOTE

If something sounds too good to be true, it probably is, and eBay Stores are no exception. Although eBay Stores makes it easy to sell items online, the ease of use comes at the expense of customizability. As you'll see, with eBay Stores you are afforded a certain amount of customization, but your store will still have a very eBay-like look and feel. If you want a completely unique store that can be tailored to your particular aesthetic tastes, you'll need to build your own online storefront from the ground up, as discussed in Chapter 4.

Additionally, eBay Stores does not provide payment processing. As with regular eBay auctions, the seller indicates how he'll accept payment—checks, money orders, PayPal, and so on—and withholds shipping the goods until payment has been rendered. With the online storefront in Chapter 4, PayPal automatically handles payment collection. With eBay Stores this is now your responsibility as the store owner.

Creating and Customizing Your eBay Store

The first step in selling online using an eBay Store is to create your eBay Store. To do so visit the eBay Stores home page at http://stores.eBay.com and find and click the button in the upper right-hand corner titled Open a Store. This prompts you to log in to eBay. If you already have an eBay account, go ahead and enter your username and password; if not, take a moment to create a free eBay account.

The first step in creating your eBay Store is selecting your store's appearance. Figure 5.1 shows a screenshot of the Select Theme screen, which presents a number of store format options. You can simply choose one of these prebuilt templates or, if you'd rather, specify a particular color scheme for a default template. (This option is at the bottom of the screen and not shown in Figure 5.1.)

After selecting a template you are prompted to provide your store's name, a description, and a logo. Take care when choosing your store's name because this name will be how customers can visit your site. The way your store's URL is decided is the store's name with spaces replaced with hyphens (-) and punctuation removed.

FIGURE 5.1

Pick a template for your eBay Store.

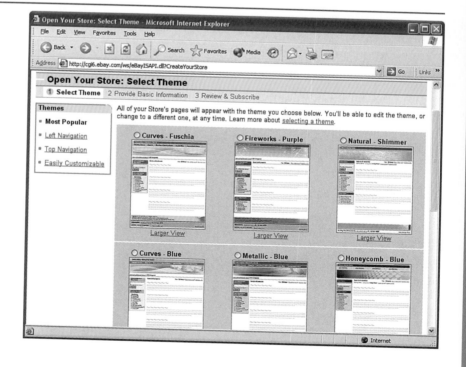

The description, as you might have guessed, provides a summary of your store. For your store's logo you can choose one of the available clip art images eBay provides, or, if you had a logo created for your store by a graphic artist, you can upload that logo to eBay's servers. I opted to use eBay's preexisting logo for Books, as Figure 5.2 shows.

The final step in creating your eBay Store is selecting the subscription level, as shown in Figure 5.3. Three subscription levels are available, each with different features:

► **Basic Store**—Ideal for beginning sellers interested in learning more about eBay Stores, this account provides a basic set of features ideal for low-volume sellers. At $15.95 it's the most affordable option, and, if you decide you need to upgrade to a more professional plan in the future, you can do so then. I'd recommend that you choose this option because it comes with a 30-day money back trial period.

► **Featured Store**—Featured stores have access to all of eBay's services that other sellers must pay for. This includes things such as eBay's Selling Manager Pro and advanced traffic and sales reports. Additionally, featured stores gain increased exposure by occasionally appearing on the eBay Stores home page. The cost per month for a featured store is $49.95.

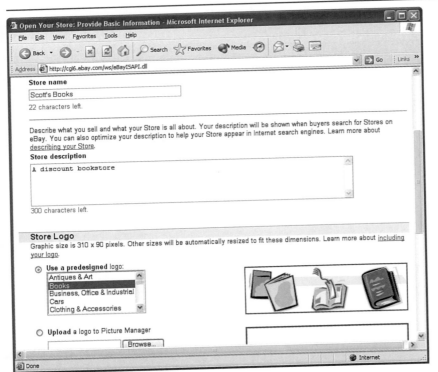

FIGURE 5.2

Choose a name, description, and logo for your store.

▶ **Anchor Store**—At nearly $500 per month it's clear that anchor stores are designed for high-volume, professional online sellers. Anchor stores come with all the benefits of featured stores along with exposure on eBay's home page.

After you choose your subscription option and click the Start My Subscription Now button, your eBay Store will be created. Don't let the monthly fees stop you from trying out eBay Stores. Both the basic and featured stores offer a 30-day money back trial.

Congratulations! At this point you have successfully created your own eBay Store. Of course your store is currently empty; you've yet to add any items for sale. You'll see how to add items to your eBay Store in the next section, "Adding Products to Your eBay Store," but before that you'll want to customize your store.

Managing Your Store

After you have created your eBay Store, you can manage the store by clicking on the Manage Store link from your My eBay page. To reach the My eBay page, simply click the My eBay button located at the top of any page (the button is circled in Figure 5.4). Then, from the My eBay page, you'll find a Manage My Store link in the left-hand column. Clicking this takes you to the Manage My Store page, shown in Figure 5.4.

IDEA GALLERY

http://shop.securewebs.com/store/

LOOKING FOR A WEB HOSTING SITE—SHOP AROUND

There are some great sites out there for hosting your website. We found SecureWebs to have a range of services and an online catalog of features. Shop around for the best deal and the types of services that you want. You may only need a small amount of space for a family or hobby website, which you can usually get from your Internet provider. Most accounts offer FTP access and a 50–100 MB of space for your own little website. But if you want to create a larger website, especially one that involves selling products or services, you might want to let a hosting site do most of the work for you. These sites take care of mass emailing, shopping carts, online catalogs, and newsletters for you. They also have security for your site, which can be difficult to program by yourself if you're a beginner. They have firewalls to prevent hackers from destroying your website as well as SSL (Secure Sockets Layer) that allows your visitors to perform transactions in a secure environment.

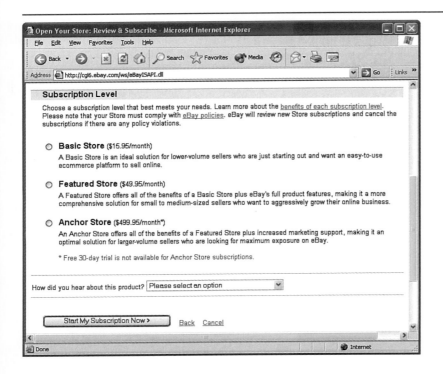

FIGURE 5.3
Select your eBay Store
subscription level.

The Manage My Store page is divided into two portions: a left-hand column with links to customize your store's settings and a summary of your store in the main portion of the page. As Figure 5.4 shows, the summary lists your subscription level, how many active listings are in your store, whether a listing header is used, and your email marketing campaigns. The listing header and email marketing information summarizes data configurable through the eBay Stores marketing tools. You'll learn about these tools later in this chapter in the "Taking Advantage of Marketing Tools" section.

For now, pay particular attention to the left-hand column. This contains a bevy of links that, when clicked, allow you to configure a particular part of your store. For example, under the Store Design heading, if you click the Display Settings link you are taken to a page where you can change the store name, description, logo, and theme you selected when creating your store.

FIGURE 5.4

Configure your store through the Manage My Store page.

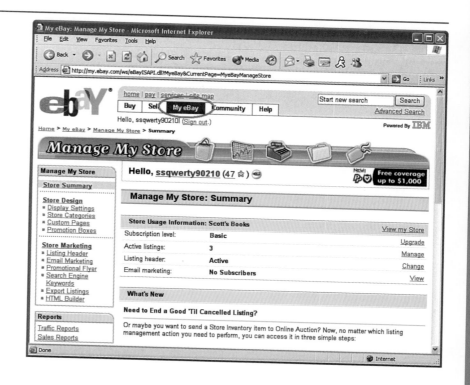

NOTE

In addition to the Store Design links there are a number of other settings that you'll learn about in future sections of this chapter. For example, the Store Marketing settings are discussed in the "Taking Advantage of Marketing Tools" section. The Reports links—Traffic Reports and Sales Reports—are discussed in the "Sales and Traffic Reports" section also later in this chapter.

One setting that you should take a moment to configure is Store Categories. When adding items to your eBay Store you'll be prompted to select what category the items belong to; then, when someone views your store, she can optionally view just the products that belong to a particular category. For this reason I encourage you to add categories to your store prior to adding items for sale.

To specify your store's categories start by clicking on the Store Categories link under the Store Design heading. You should then see a page similar to the one shown in Figure 5.5 listing your store's categories. From this screen you can reorder the categories or rename them. To rename a category click the Edit Category Names link in the upper right-hand corner. To reorder a category, simply click the up or down arrow to the right of the category to adjust its position.

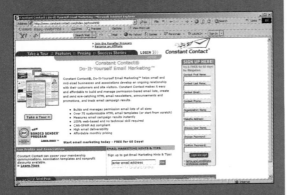

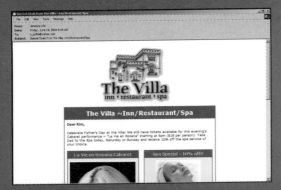

NEWSLETTERS 101

Depending on the type of website you develop, you may want to send email newsletters to people who register on your site. There are all kinds of things to consider when you're going to build a list and email people.

1) How many email blasts can I send from my Internet provider? Is there a limit?

2) How do I prevent my messages from being filtered as spam?

3) How do I know if people are even opening my messages?

4) Should I create text-based messages or HTML messages?

5) What is the most effective way to communicate with people via email?

FIGURE 5.5

Create a few categories for your store before adding items for sale.

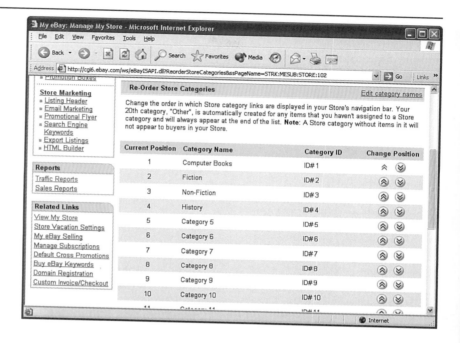

Adding Products to Your eBay Store

Now that you have your eBay Store set up, the next step is to list the inventory you have for sale. To add an item to your eBay Store click on the Sell button at the top of any page on eBay. This takes you to the Sell page (shown in Figure 5.6) .

Note that there are four ways to sell your item:

NOTE

A discussion of selling real estate on eBay is beyond the scope of this book.

- ▶ As an online auction
- ▶ At a fixed price
- ▶ As store inventory
- ▶ Real estate

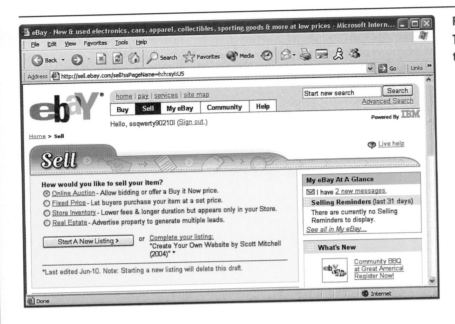

FIGURE 5.6
To list items for sale, click the Sell button.

When listing an item using an online auction, you provide a starting bid price and auction duration. During the auction's duration users can bid on the item with the highest bidder winning the item. For example, imagine that I wanted to sell a copy of my book *Teach Yourself ASP.NET in 24 Hours* using my eBay Store with the auction format. I might decide to make the starting price $5.00 and the duration seven days. After I completed listing this item, the auction would begin, and, over the next seven days, users could place bids on the book. What's nice about listing an item using the online auction is that the item appears in both your eBay Store *and* the main eBay website. That is, if someone searches eBay for *ASP.NET* my auction will appear in the search results. This auction also shows up when someone visits my eBay Store directly.

Although auctions can lead to competitive bidding and, therefore, a higher sales price, many sellers don't like the uncertainty of an auction. Instead, they'd rather just list the item for a fixed price. As with online auctions, fixed price items are listed for a specified duration, and items added using the fixed price option will appear in *both* your eBay Store and the general eBay listings.

Having your items listed in both your eBay Store and in eBay's general site listings may seem like a good way to spread the word about your store. Although this is definitely true, keep in mind that eBay does charge a premium for listing items in its general section. If, instead, you want to merely list the item in your eBay Store and *not* in the general eBay listings, you can do so by selecting to add your item as store inventory. Although having an item listed just in your eBay Store will provide less visibility for your inventory, it does cost substantially less than listing it in eBay's general listings and can be listed for longer durations. For example, listing a book with a fixed price of $9.99 in eBay's general listings and your eBay Store costs $0.35 for a seven day listing; the same book can be listed in just your eBay Store for $0.02 for 30 days.

> *"Having your items listed in both your eBay Store and in eBay's general site listings may seem like a good way to spread the word about your store. Although this is definitely true, keep in mind that eBay does charge a premium for listing items in its general section."*

After you decide how your item will be listed, adding the item is virtually identical to the process for adding a normal auctioned item. The only difference is that when you have an eBay Store, when adding an item for sale you are prompted to select what category you want the item to be listed under in your eBay Store.

After you complete the listing process, the item will automatically be added to your eBay Store, and—if you select to list the item using the online auction or fixed price options—it will also appear in eBay's general listings. Figure 5.7 shows my eBay Store with several books listed for sale.

A FEW WORDS ABOUT CSS—CASCADING STYLE SHEETS

If you're going to be a professional web developer, you'll eventually want to move away from tables and start implementing CSS. Adactio was the best place we found to help you make this leap. There are many resources out on the Web to help you. Mezzoblue is great, too (http://www.mezzoblue.com/css/crib-sheet/). We chose Adactio, though, because this site's designer took the time to create a really great introduction into the discipline of CSS. He takes you through the Web that you already know and into the future of web design with style sheets. He explains why it's a good thing to separate your content from your layout and structure. In the end, you'll find that CSS may take some planning and a little more setup time, but the results are worth the effort. In a nutshell, here's what he says:

"Just imagine all the benefits that come with separating your presentation from your content.

"Your pages will be smaller, much smaller. Without the bloat that comes with nested tables, spacer images and font tags, your markup will be leaner and meaner. That will appeal to search engines.

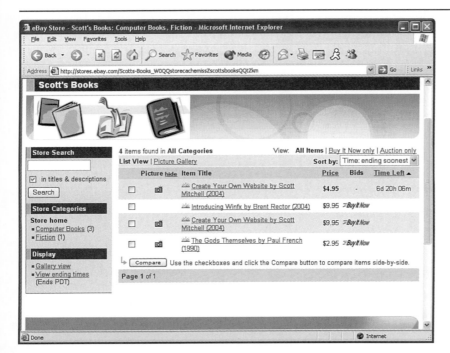

FIGURE 5.7
Each item listed appears in your eBay store.

This is the main page of my eBay Store, which lists items for sale across all categories ordered by the items' ending times. In the left-hand portion of my store there's a search box that potential customers can use to search for items within my store. Beneath that is the list of categories that have items for sale. By clicking a category link, the visitor sees those items for sale in that category.

NOTE

After adding a new item it may take several minutes before the item appears within your eBay Store.

Collecting Payments and Order Fulfillment

After you have added items to your eBay Store the next step is, unfortunately, a bit out of your control. You must now wait for customers to come and buy your products! eBay offers a variety of marketing tools to help bring potential customers to your eBay Store; these tools are discussed in the next section, "Taking Advantage of Marketing Tools." But for now let's assume that you have a customer at your store who's interested in making a purchase. What's the process, from a user's purchase and payment to order fulfillment?

How the customer makes the purchase depends on how the item for sale was listed. If the item was listed as an online auction, the customer may make a bid on the item, but the item is not actually purchased by that customer until the auction ends, at which point the customer with the highest bid receives the item. (When creating an auction you can, optionally, add a Buy It Now price, which allows an interested customer to prematurely end the auction by agreeing to buy the item at the Buy It Now price.)

If the item being purchased was listed as a fixed price item or added to the store inventory, the user agrees to pay the item's price, thereby purchasing the item immediately.

Keep in mind that eBay Stores does not handle payment processing. eBay Stores simply provides an easy way to list items for sale and a way for a customer to specify that she wants to buy a particular item. Collecting payment, however, falls squarely on your shoulders, the eBay Store owner. When listing an item for sale, you are prompted to select what methods of payment you accept—PayPal, credit cards, personal checks, money orders, and so on. When a buyer agrees to purchase one of your items, you and the buyer must coordinate to have payment made. This might involve giving the buyer an address to mail a money order or information on how to deposit funds into your PayPal account.

After an item's purchase is completed—that is, either after a fixed price item has been bought or an auction has ended with a winning bidder—you will receive an email informing you of the purchase, and the item will be automatically deducted from your online store's inventory. (When adding items to your store you can indicate how much inventory you have of that particular item. When the inventory runs out, the item will be removed completely from your eBay Store.)

Upon receiving email notification that a sale has been made, you and the buyer must now collaborate to finalize payment. After you receive the buyer's payment, it is your responsibility to ship the purchased item. After you've received payment and shipped the goods, the transaction is complete. Congratulations!

Taking Advantage of Marketing Tools

As any businessperson knows, having the best products available for the lowest prices around means absolutely nothing if no customers visit your store. Collectively, businesses spend billions of dollars a year on advertising, letting you know they exist, encouraging you to visit their stores. Ads in the yellow pages or newspapers, radio spots, and billboards are all mediums used by traditional businesses to drive potential customers to their doors. With online businesses, however, attracting customers involves the same techniques but utilizes different tools.

To aid with your marketing efforts eBay Stores provides a number of marketing tools. These marketing tools can be found in the Manage My Store page and are listed in the left-hand column under the Store Marketing link (see Figure 5.8).

WHAT DO YOU DO IF A TRANSACTION GOES SOUR?

Because payment processing and order fulfillment are handled between individuals—you and the buyer—rather than having eBay act as a proxy, a justified concern of many buyers and sellers is what happens when a deal goes south? What happens if a buyer promises to buy a product of yours, but, after weeks of waiting, he's yet to provide payment? Or what if you can't get in touch with the winning bidder of an auction to provide instructions on paying?

eBay addresses these problems in a myriad of ways. The first approach is through *feedback*. Whenever a transaction completes, buyers and sellers are strongly encouraged to provide feedback of the transaction. This gives future buyers and sellers an indication of the trustworthiness of the person whom they're considering buying from or selling to. In fact, a number of eBay options—such as adding a Buy It Now price to an auction—require a minimum seller feedback rating.

Of course, regardless of one's feedback, problems or disputes may arise. eBay provides mediation options, insurance, and refunds for a variety of problems. For more information on these programs, along with tips for both buyers and sellers, visit the eBay Security & Resolution Center at http://pages.ebay.com/securitycenter/.

These marketing tools include

- **Listing headers**—Add a link back to your eBay Store in all your item descriptions. This provides instant exposure to your eBay Store for those who search and find your listings through eBay's general listings.

- **Email marketing**—When visiting your store, customers can sign up for your store's newsletter. You can then send out targeted messages to those who have signed up, alerting your interested clientele of sales and specials.

- **Promotional flyers**—When shipping a purchased item to a customer you can include a promotional flyer along with the item. This flyer, which eBay Stores can help you generate, can inform the buyer of additional items on your store he might be interested in.

- **Search engine keywords**—Each page in your eBay store contains special HTML elements that help search engines find and categorize your eBay Store. You can customize these keywords for each page in your eBay Store.

These marketing tools can be used to help promote your site and attract new customers. Before you begin using these tools, however, I encourage you to first work on building up your store's inventory. After your store is well stocked and ready for business, it's time to start marketing, but not before then.

FIGURE 5.8

Promote your eBay Store with a wealth of marketing tools.

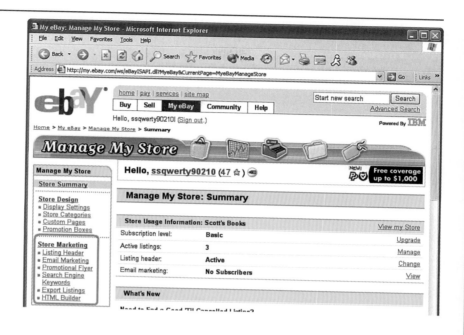

Sales and Traffic Reports

After you've stocked your store and started attracting customers through your marketing efforts, you can take a moment to breathe a sigh of relief and give yourself a well-deserved pat on the back. However, running your own online business is not for the weak or weary, and even a store that's selling well could always sell better. One way to maximize your sales is to analyze current and past sales and trends in your store.

Is a particular type of item selling better than another? If so, maybe you need to do a better job marketing the other type. Or perhaps you need to stop selling the other type of item altogether and focus like a laser on your top-selling items. Traffic trends can illustrate how users are browsing your site—are they arriving

through searching eBay's general listings or through search engines? Is there a particular page that has the lion's share of the page views? If so, do you have links to your top-selling items from that popular page?

To be able to perform such analyses, it's imperative that you have the necessary data. eBay Stores provides this important data through Traffic Reports and Sales Reports, both of which are available from the left-hand column of the Manage My Store page.

Inspecting Your Site's Traffic

Each time a visitor visits a web page on your eBay Store, that information is saved by eBay. This information can then be examined at a later date to analyze information about your site's traffic. You can see what pages are the most popular and how customers are finding your eBay Store.

To view your store's Traffic Report simply click the Traffic Report link from the Manage My Store page's left-hand column. The eBay Stores Traffic Report is hosted by a third-party company separate from eBay. When viewing your Traffic Report you will be notified of this fact and must agree to the privacy terms presented. After you have done this, you'll be taken to the report.

As Figure 5.9 shows, this report lists the daily number of page views, the number of unique visits, the number of home page views for the current month, and the most popular pages all for the current month. More detailed reports are available in the Your Key Reports section, and additional reports are available from the Traffic Reports menu in the left-hand column. These additional reports can show you what the most popular search terms in your store are along with how people are arriving at your site: through search engines, through links in other websites, or through eBay's general listings.

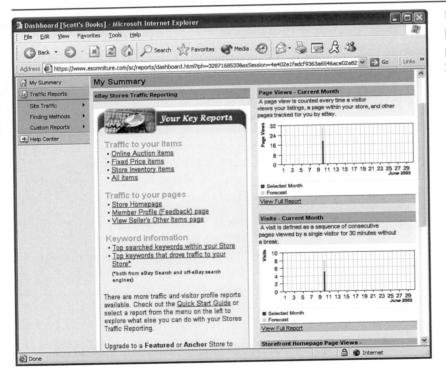

FIGURE 5.9

Inspect the traffic patterns of your eBay Store.

SALES AND TRAFFIC REPORTS

Your eBay Store's Traffic Reports won't be of interest until your store has been around for a number of months. It's not until this point that the reports will illustrate any sort of patterns or show any trends that can be used to fine-tune your marketing. As you can see in Figure 5.9, the data is pretty sparse, as this is the Traffic Report for my relatively new eBay Store.

Tracking Sales

In the day-to-day grind of selling online you are focused on adding new items to your store, receiving payment, and shipping those items already sold. You are more concerned with the latest emergency—a buyer says his product never arrived!—instead of having a more global view of your store's sales. However, to properly market your store, you need to, at some point, have a good grasp of the overall sales trends for your store. Is a certain type of product vastly outselling another? Do you see a large spike in sales the week after sending out an email through the eBay Stores email marketing tool?

> "To properly market your store, you need to, at some point, have a good grasp of the overall sales trends for your store."

This high-level view of your sales can help you focus your attention, money, and energy into increasing sales and determining what marketing techniques are leading to successful sales. To view the Sales Report simply click the Sales Report link in the Manage My Store page. At this point, you may be prompted whether you want to sign up for the Basic Sales reporting

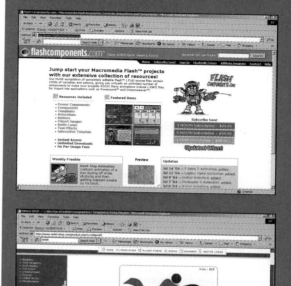

package or the Sales Plus package. Sales Plus is free to those with an eBay Store, so choose the Sales Plus option.

The Sales Report, shown in Figure 5.10, can be customized to view sales for a particular month or week, showing the total number of sales and average sales price. If you are selling items using the auction model you may be interested to learn whether there is any correlation between the duration or ending date of the auction and the ending sales price. The Sales Report can assist in this analysis because you can view sales by duration and sales by ending day or time.

As with the Traffic Reports, the Sales Reports are really only useful after you have had

enough sales to extract meaning from the data. After your store has been established and at least several weeks have passed with sales, I would encourage you to view your store's Sales Reports at least once a month, looking for trends or other interesting bits of information that may help you sell better.

> **TIP**
>
> The Sales Report also shows how much in eBay fees you are paying on a monthly or weekly basis. You can use this data to keep track of your store's overhead.

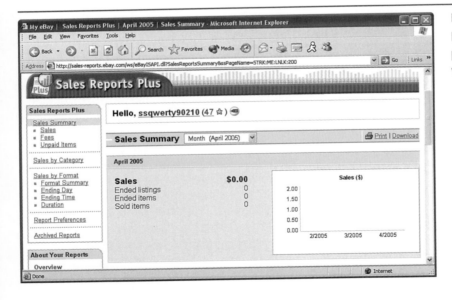

FIGURE 5.10

Put your finger on the pulse of your store's sales with the Sales Report.

Summary

From books to clothes to electronics to DVDs, millions of people are buying merchandise online. If you are ready to take your business online, you have two options for selling your product: use a custom built online storefront website, as examined in Chapter 4, or create your own eBay Store. A customized website gives you much greater flexibility over the look and feel of your site and also can integrate payment processing using PayPal, but eBay Stores makes the process of adding inventory to your online store much simpler.

Additionally, eBay Stores comes equipped with a user-friendly interface. If your customers are already among the millions of eBay users, they'll find the buying process on your store to be familiar. Also, because your store is located on eBay, your store's inventory can also be added to the general eBay listings, increasing the likelihood of new customers finding your store.

eBay Stores also offers a variety of tools to help market your store, including tools for sending emails to interested customers and printing out promotional flyers that can be included when shipping customers their purchased products. Along with these marketing tools there are also reports to view your store's traffic and sales histories. eBay provides a plethora of tools to make your online business a successful venture.

CHAPTER 6

Creating a Blog with Blogger

In the early days of the World Wide Web, publishing content online required a level of technical know-how common only among computer experts. This has changed over the years, though, thanks to a variety of tools and programs that have made publishing online a simple task. As this book has shown, creating your own website is as easy as formatting a document with a word processor program such as Microsoft Word.

Even though this book provides a number of website templates and software to easily customize them, creating your own website could be even simpler still. Creating your own website involves two steps:

1. Procuring your website. As discussed in Chapter 2, "Creating a Website," this involves contacting your ISP or a web host provider, as well as registering a domain name.

2. Creating the site's content. Chapter 3, "Creating a Family/Person Website," and Chapter 4, "Creating an Online Storefront," showed how to modify the provided website templates to create the pages that make up your site.

In talking with readers, most have found the first step to be an administrative nuisance, one that they might not feel technologically comfortable with. Although there are readers who find learning about the inner plumbing of the Internet interesting and exciting, most simply want to build their site and share it with the world. For those who want to quickly and easily publish content on the web without having to work with a web host provider or register a domain name, a *blog* might be more suitable.

A blog is a sort of online journal, a website whose content can easily be added to by the blog's creator. With a blog you do not have to create your own website or register a domain name; rather, your blog is hosted on an existing company's website. Blogs strive to make setting up, configuring, customizing, and adding content to the blog as simple as possible. As you'll see in this chapter, all facets of working with a blog can be handled through a web browser. You don't need to use Mozilla Composer to customize or add new content to your blog, just Internet Explorer or any other web browser.

Although blogs are easy to create and update, they are really an ideal option only for sites whose visitors are interested in just the most recent additions to the site. Typically, a blog's home page will list the 10 or 15 most recent entries made to the blog. Whenever you add a new blog entry through the web-based interface, that entry will be automatically added to the blog's home page, replacing the oldest entry on the home page.

For this reason you probably wouldn't want to use a blog for an organizational site or eCommerce site. For these types of sites you likely want to have more control over the site's home page and don't want older content to necessarily drop off the front page. Blogs are a great choice, though, for family/personal sites. Many people use blogs as an online journal, one that can be added to from any computer with a connection to the Internet and can be viewed by anyone in the world.

A number of companies offer blogs, and these companies' offerings vary on the price and features provided. Although each company's blogs provide different feature sets, in general blogs typically provide the following features:

▶ A way for visitors to the blog to view the most recent content, as well as older, archived content.

▶ An easy, quick way for you, the blog creator, to add new content to the blog.

▶ A means for you to customize the appearance of the blog.

This chapter shows how to build a blog using Blogger.com, illustrating how these features are provided.

What Do You Blog About?

Over the past few years the popularity of blogging has exploded. A study done in 2005 estimates that there are nearly 10 *million* blogs online, with more than 10,000 new blogs being created each day! Blogs are so popular because they enable anyone, regardless of computer skills, to become an online publisher with just the click of a mouse.

Most individuals use blogs as an online diary, sharing glimpses into their daily lives. Others create blogs focused on a particular topic, such as the latest happenings of their favorite sports team or commentary on local politics. Even businesses are getting into blogs as a means to communicate more intimately with their customers. For example, at http://blog.ford.com you'll find the 2005 Ford Mustang Blog, a blog contributed to by the Mustang's design team during the design and construction of the car. Popular search engine Google keeps surfers aware of their latest offerings through their company's blog, available at http://www.google.com/googleblog/.

Before creating your own blog take a moment to first decide what your blog will be about. Will you use your blog as an online journal to share with friends and family? Will you focus on a particular topic? If you run a business, might a blog be a useful marketing tool for communicating with current and prospective customers?

TIP

Two maladies can ruin any blog: stale content and off-topic content. Visitors to your blog are interested in recent entries and will be put off if they see that your last entry was from six months ago. Similarly, if you are creating a blog focused on a particular topic, try your best to refrain from making off-topic entries. Folks who visit a focused blog do so because they are interested in that topic; don't frustrate your readers by delving into tangential topics.

Creating a Blog

The first step in creating a blog is deciding what company to use. There are a variety of companies in the blog space, each boasting different features and pricing plans. Some companies offer a free basic service and charge for premium features; others provide no free plans, but do offer a free trial period for their services. Some of the major blog providers (to name just a few) are

▶ Blogger (http://www.Blogger.com)

▶ LiveJournal (http://www.LiveJournal.com)

▶ SquareSpace (http://www.SquareSpace.com)

▶ MyBlogSite (http://www.MyBlogSite.com)

▶ MovableType (http://www.SixApart.com/movabletype/)

ADS ON YOUR SITE?

What if your site becomes pretty popular? You might want to consider putting ads, like Google Ads, on your site to bring extra revenue. Google's AdSense delivers advertising that is targeted to customers who like your content. You receive revenue any time a visitor from your site clicks through to one of the ads in the Google sidebar. Google ads are tastefully done—no big flashing ads or pop-ups that annoy your visitors.

There are tons of ways to make money from your website even if you don't sell anything. Check out the site called Web Marketing Today (http://www.wilsonweb.com/wmta/adrev-8steps.htm).

This chapter shows how to create a blog using Blogger. I chose Blogger because it offers a free basic blog package that provides a nice mix of features and ease of use. When creating your first blog, I encourage you to follow along and use Blogger, but afterward, if you are not satisfied with the user experience offered by Blogger, feel free to explore the other blog providers.

To get started, fire up your web browser of choice and visit Blogger's home page, http://www.Blogger.com (see Figure 6.1). To create a new Blogger account, simply click the Create Your Blog Now arrow in the bottom right-hand corner.

NOTE

The upper right-hand corner of the Blogger home page contains the sign-in interface for those who have already created a Blogger account. After you have created your blog on Blogger and want to add content to the blog, you'll need to visit the Blogger home page and enter your username and password into the appropriate text boxes.

Clicking the Create Your Blog Now arrow takes you through three screens that prompt you for various account creation information. The first screen, shown in Figure 6.2, asks for account information. From this screen you need to choose a username and password to use to sign in to Blogger and update your blog. You're also asked to choose a display name, which will appear after each blog entry.

FIGURE 6.1

Create a new blog from
the Blogger home
page.

FIGURE 6.2

Choose a username,
password, and display
name.

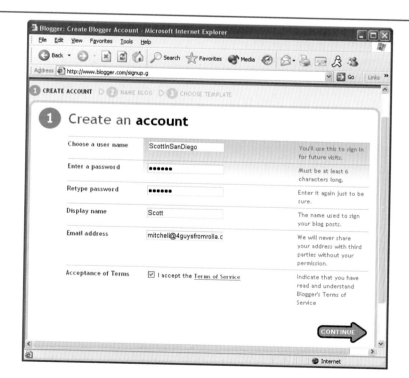

The second screen in the blog creation process asks for information specific to your blog, such as your blog's title and the URL you want to use for your blog (see Figure 6.3). The blog title will appear at the top of your blog's home page. For this chapter, I will create a blog that provides information about local events happening in San Diego and have decided to give my blog the title, "San Diego Events."

The Blog Address (URL) field indicates the URL to your blog. Note that by default your blog will be hosted on Blogger's web servers at the domain name http://*YourBlogName*.blogspot.com. If you already have a public web server available that supports FTP access, you can configure your blog to be hosted on your own web server by clicking on the Advanced Blog Setup link and following the instructions. For my "San Diego Events" blog, I chose the name ScottInSanDiego, meaning that my blog is publicly available to anyone in the world with an Internet connection at http://ScottInSanDiego.blogspot.com.

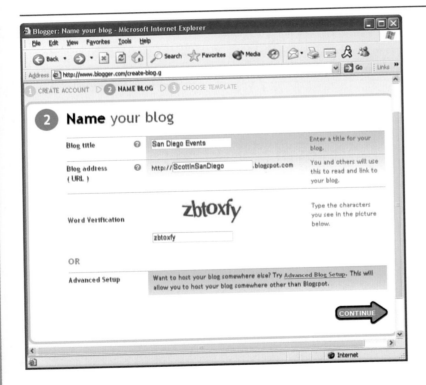

FIGURE 6.3

Choose a title and address for your blog.

The last screen in the setup process allows you to choose the template used for your blog. As you can see in Figure 6.4, Blogger offers a number of templates. For my blog I've chosen the Sand Dollar template, but feel free to pick a template that matches your personal aesthetic taste and style.

After you have selected a template, click the Continue arrow to complete the setup process. Congratulations! At this point, you now have your own blog. In the remainder of this chapter we'll look at how to add new content to your blog as well as how to customize the look and feel.

NOTE

We'll examine how to switch an existing blog's template, as well as how to customize a selected template, in the "Customizing the Blog's Template" section at the end of this chapter.

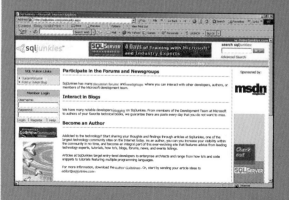

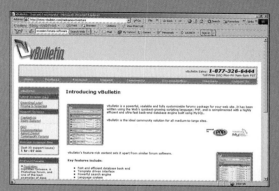

GREAT COMMUNITY SITE

If you're going to have a community website, then you have to tell people how to participate in your community. This site does a great job of telling visitors how they can interact with the rest of the community through blogs, discussion forums, newsgroups, and authoring articles.

If you click around their website, you'll find their discussion forum page that offers around 50 discussions. So how do you get a discussion page like that one? If you're reading this book, the best idea is to purchase discussion software from a company that has done all of the programming for you. VBulletin (www.vbulletin.com) is a pretty good discussion software that isn't too expensive—$85 annually for one server.

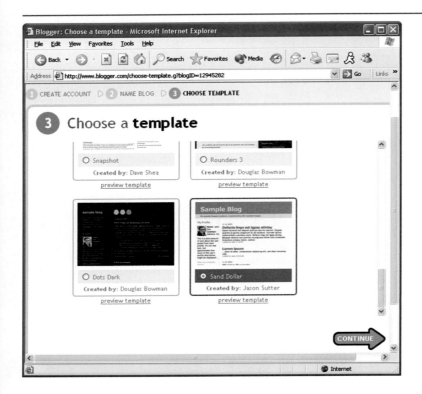

FIGURE 6.4

Customize the appearance of your blog by selecting one of the provided templates.

Adding Content to Your Blog

Immediately after creating your new account you will see a Start Posting arrow that, if clicked, takes you to your blog's administration page. The administration page is a web page accessible only by you, the blog's creator. From the administration page you can post new content, edit existing content, and customize your blog's settings. You can reach this administrative page at any time by visiting the Blogger home page—http://www.Blogger.com—and logging in with the username and password you chose when creating your account.

Figure 6.5 shows a screenshot of the administration page. Notice that the administration page has four tabs along the top of the page:

- Posting—Allows you to add new posts to your blog or edit existing posts.
- Settings—Allows you to configure your blog's configuration settings.
- Template—Enables advanced users to customize their blog's appearance.
- View Blog—Opens a new browser window showing your blog's home page.

FIGURE 6.5

Only you, the blog creator, can access your blog's administration page.

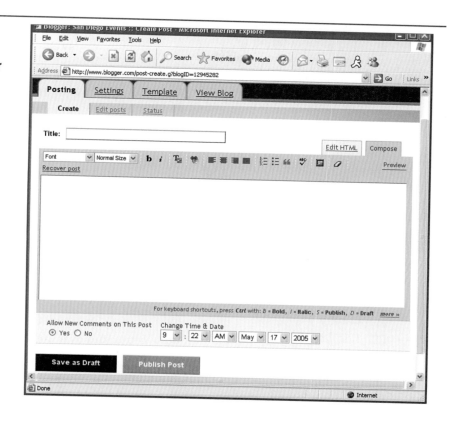

We'll examine the Settings and Template tabs in the next section, "Customizing Your Blog." For now, though, let's focus on the Posting tab.

Clicking on the Posting tab loads the Posting user interface, which is the interface shown in Figure 6.5. Notice that underneath the Posting tab are three additional subtabs relating to posting actions:

▶ Create—To add a new entry, click on the Create tab. This loads the interface shown in Figure 6.5, allowing you to add a new entry to your blog.

▶ Edit Posts—Clicking this tab lists the existing entries in your blog, allowing you to edit or delete past content.

▶ Status—This tab's interface shows the status of the last posting action. For example, when making a new post, if there are any errors or any problem in saving the post, such information will be available through the Status tab.

Now that you are familiar with the Posting tab, it's time to create your first blog entry. Each blog entry includes a title and the actual content of the entry. As Figure 6.5 showed, the Create subtab interface has two text boxes: one for the blog entry's title and one for the actual content of the entry.

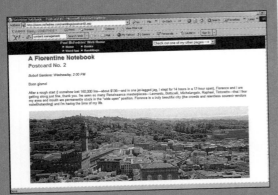

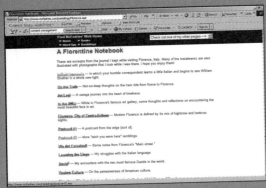

AWESOME PERSONAL JOURNAL

A great way to share vacation memories is to put your journal on your website. It doesn't have to be complicated. Just set up an index page and add entries as individual pages as you write them. Paul McFedries (one of Sams's authors) created a journal from his trip to Italy. The entries are fun to read and filled with pictures from his visit. He incorporated links to other entries or to whatever he was writing about for further information—a nice touch. This is a great site to study if you're looking for examples of good writing. Anyone can put vacation pictures on their website and tell friends what they did each day. But Paul's writing makes you feel like you're reading an insider's guide to Italy. His site is fun to read even if you don't know him.

The title can only be plain, unformatted text, but the content can be formatted to a much higher degree. The text box for the blog entry's content allows you to optionally select a font, a font size, whether you want the text to be bold or italic, the text's color and justification, and so on. You can also easily turn selected text into a hyperlink to another website or web page. The formatting of the text can be controlled through the formatting options along the top of the blog entry text box (this formatting toolbar is circled in Figure 6.6).

Adding and formatting a blog entry's content is similar to typing and formatting a letter in a word processor program such as Microsoft Word. Figure 6.6 shows a screenshot of the blog entry screen after I have added a new entry.

Notice that I have certain text in **bold**, such as **attracting over 100,000 San Diegans** and **Jane Q. Doe**; the quote from Jane Q. Doe is in *italics*. Also, I've changed the text color of PB Block Party to red and linked Discover Pacific Beach to the website http://www.pacificbeach.org.

Specifying these format settings for your blog entry's content is straightforward. Simply use the mouse to select the text you want to apply the formatting to and then click the appropriate formatting icon in the toolbar. For example, to have the text Discover Pacific Beach link to http://www.pacificbeach.org, I first selected the text and then clicked the link button in the toolbar (the picture of a globe with a chain link, to the right of the text color icon and to the left of the left align icon). This displayed a dialog box that prompted me for the URL that the user should be taken to when the link is clicked, into which I entered http://www.pacificbeach.org (see Figure 6.7).

FIGURE 6.6

Enter a new, nicely formatted blog entry through the Posting tab.

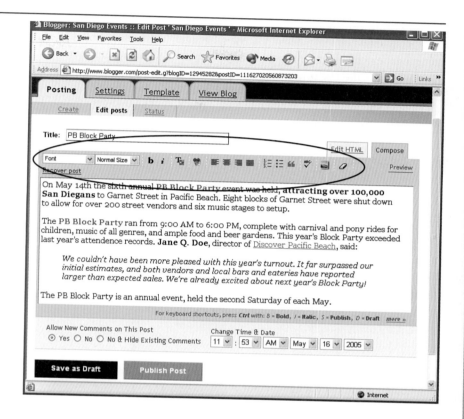

FIGURE 6.7

Add a hyperlink by selecting the text to link and clicking the hyperlink icon.

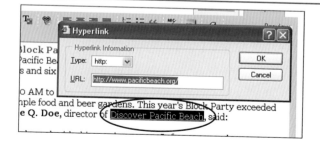

In addition to specifying the title and content for a blog entry, you can also indicate whether comments are allowed for the blog entry and the date and time the blog entry was made. (These settings can be found immediately beneath the blog entry content text box near the bottom of the page.) If comments are allowed, any visitor to your blog may leave a comment for the blog entry. The date and time setting, which defaults to the current date and time, is simply displayed next to the blog entry on the home page.

Finally, to publish your blog entry, click the Publish Post button at the bottom of the page. This takes you to the Status tab, informing you of the status of the posting. Figure 6.8 shows the Status tab after I published the PB Block Party entry.

FIGURE 6.8

Publishing your blog entry is as simple as clicking a button!

TIP

If you aren't yet ready to publish your blog entry but don't want to lose the content you've already entered, you can click the Save as Draft button. This saves a copy of your blog entry but does not yet publish it to the blog's home page. This saved draft can be found and edited later through the Edit Posts tab.

After you publish a blog entry it appears automatically on your blog's home page. You can visit your blog by clicking the View Blog tab in the administration interface. Figure 6.9 shows a screenshot of my blog's home page after the PB Block Party entry is added. Whereas the administration page is accessible only by you, the blog's creator, *anyone* can view your blog's home page.

THE PURPOSE OF THE DATE AND TIME SETTINGS

Because Blogger lets you supply a blog entry date and time, you may naturally think that by setting the date and time to a future date, you would be able to have the blog entry not appear in your blog's home page until the specified date and time. However, this is not how the date and time setting is used. After you publish a blog entry, the entry appears automatically in your blog, regardless of the date and time setting.

The date and time setting is used in two ways: first, on the blog home page each blog entry's date and time published are shown. This date and time is precisely the date and time setting you specify; second, as the number of entries in your blog content continues to grow, Blogger automatically starts listing links in the blog home page to view older entries, ones that have slipped off the home page. These links to older entries are listed by month and year. Therefore, when the user opts to see past entries for, say, August 2005, Blogger displays those blog entries whose date and time were set to fall within that month.

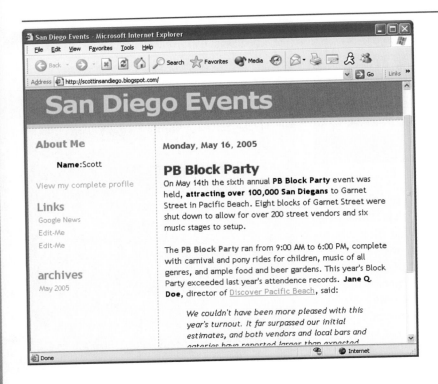

FIGURE 6.9
My blog's home page now contains my latest blog entry.

Customizing Your Blog

As you saw in the "Adding Content to Your Blog" section earlier in the chapter, Blogger makes it easy to add and edit blog entries. Additionally, Blogger makes it just as easy to customize your blog. Through the Settings tab you can specify your blog's title and description, how various portions of the blog are formatted, whether your blog allows readers to add comments, how frequently to archive content, and a plethora of other options. In this section we'll examine the gaggle of customizations offered through the Settings tab.

To begin, start by clicking on the Settings tab in the blog's administration page. The Settings tab has eight subtabs:

- **Basic**—The Basic tab includes rudimentary blog settings. Here you can specify your blog's title and description, along with whether you want your blog added to the official Blogger blog listings and other settings.

- **Publishing**—Blogger allows you to host your blog on its servers (through BlogSpot.com) or on your own website. The Publishing tab provides settings that specify where the blog should be hosted.

▶ **Formatting**—The Formatting tab includes settings to tweak the look and feel of your blog. You can specify how date and times should be formatted, what time zone you are publishing from, whether the title field should be shown on each blog entry, and so on.

▶ **Comments**—By default, your blog accepts comments from readers who may stop by your blog and are registered with Blogger. You can change these default settings—perhaps not allowing any comments, or allowing any reader to leave a comment—through the Comments tab.

▶ **Archiving**—Recall that your blog's home page includes only the more recent postings. Older posts are relegated to archived pages. The Archiving tab provides a means to customize how often archiving occurs.

▶ **Site Feed**—Most blogs provide a *site feed*, a file that contains the most recent blog entries. These feeds are automatically generated and can be used by programs called *blog aggregators*, allowing readers to subscribe to your blog and receive notification whenever new entries are posted. You can specify whether you want your blog to include a site feed through this tab.

▶ **Email**—One of the cooler features of Blogger is that you can, optionally, post new blog entries simply by sending an email to a specified email address. The Email tab explains how to set up this functionality. Additionally, you can configure your blog to automatically email you a copy of any blog content published on your blog.

▶ **Members**—By default, only you, the blog creator, may post new entries to your blog. However, you can allow others to post to your blog, as well. You can specify those additional people who can post to your blog through the Members tab.

Let's take a moment to examine each of these Settings subtabs in detail.

TIP

Many of the settings fields in the various subtabs have a question mark icon next to them. Clicking this icon displays a help page describing the setting's purpose. Be sure to read this help information if you get stuck!

Examining the Basic Tab

Recall that when creating your blog you were prompted to choose a title for your blog. If, at any time, you decide you want to change your blog's title you can do so through the Basic tab. As you saw in Figure 6.9, the blog's title appears at the top of the blog's home page. Figure 6.10 shows the Basic tab.

In addition to setting your blog's title, the Basic tab also provides a setting for the blog's description. The description, if provided, appears beneath the title on the blog's home page. Along with setting the title and description, the Basic tab also includes the following settings:

▶ **Add Your Blog to Our Listings?**—Blogger maintains a master list of blogs on its site. This setting indicates whether you want your blog to appear in this master listing.

▶ **Show Quick Editing on Your Blog?**—If this option is set to Yes, when logged on to Blogger and visiting your blog's home page each blog entry will have a pencil icon next to it. If you click this icon you are taken directly to the Edit Post screen.

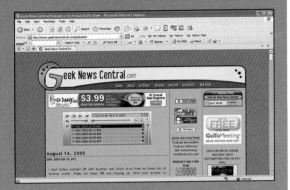

WHEN THE WRITTEN WORD JUST ISN'T ENOUGH

If you have something to say and you're a great writer, blogging is great. But if you're looking for a more avant-garde medium to communicate, try podcasting. Having a podcast is like having your own talk radio show and being able to broadcast it over the Internet for anyone to hear. Some people sing, some tell ghost stories, some recite poetry, and some just talk about whatever is on their mind. A good place to hear podcasts from other people and learn about how to create your own is Geek News Central.

▶ **Show Email Post Links?**—If this option is set to Yes, each blog entry on the blog's home page will have a mail icon next to it that any visitor can see. If a visitor clicks this icon he can email the particular blog entry to a friend.

▶ **Show Compose Mode for All Your blogs?**—This setting (off the screen in Figure 6.10) determines, when writing a new blog entry or editing an existing one, whether the WYSIWYG editor is used. Unless you are familiar with HTML, leave this option as Yes; otherwise, you'll need to write your blog entries using HTML as opposed to the word processor-like interface shown back in Figure 6.6.

At the bottom of each of the Settings subtabs you'll find a Save Settings button. After making any changes to the settings in the subtab be sure to click on Save Settings, so as to save the changes you made.

> **NOTE**
>
> When you make a change to your blog's settings and click the Save Settings button, the changes won't immediately appear on your blog's home page. Rather, you need to republish your blog. This process is discussed in detail in the "Republishing Your Blog" section later in the chapter.

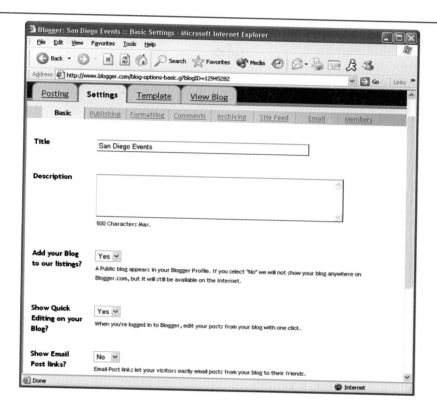

Altering the Blog's Appearance Through the Formatting Tab

Whenever you post a new entry to your blog, it appears on your blog's home page. As the number of total entries increases, the home page quickly can become cluttered. Hence Blogger allows you to specify how many posts to display on the home page. From the Formatting tab you can specify either an absolute number of posts to show on the home page, or you can opt to show all posts within a specified number of days. The Formatting tab also includes settings to indicate the date and time formats to use for headers, archive links,

and the time stamps added to each blog entry, along with the language to use for the date/time settings. You can also specify what time zone you live in, so that the time listed with each post is relative to your local time zone.

Figure 6.11 shows about half the Formatting tab's available settings. Other than the Date Language setting, those settings not shown in Figure 6.11 should simply use the default values provided.

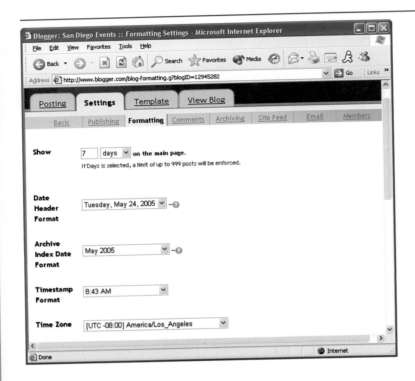

FIGURE 6.11
Alter the look of the elements on the blog's home page through the Formatting tab.

Managing Comment Settings

Although a blog allows only a specified set of users to make posts, many blogs permit readers to leave comments. Comments turn a blog from a one-way communication medium into more of a dialogue. By default, your blog can accept comments only from visitors registered with Blogger, although you can change this behavior through the Comments tab (see Figure 6.12).

By default, comments are shown, although you can opt to hide them, thereby making your blog comment free. If you decide to allow comments, you can dictate who, exactly, can leave comments, through the Who Can Comment? option. The choices are

▶ **Only Registered Users**—If this option is selected, only visitors who are registered with Blogger can leave comments on your blog. Typically people register with Blogger when they want to create their own blog, although users can register just to leave comments.

▶ **Anyone**—If this option is chosen, anyone can leave a comment on your blog.

▶ **Only Members of this Blog**—You can easily configure your blog to have additional users who can post to your blog. These special users are referred to as members and are added through the Members tab. When this option is selected in the Comments tab, only members may leave comments.

In addition to specifying who can leave comments you can also specify how the comment time stamp is formatted, whether comments are displayed on the same page as the blog entry or are shown in a new browser window, and whether profile images are shown on comments. (Profile images are images that are links back to the commenter's Blogger profile. There will only be a profile image for those who have an account with Blogger.)

Another cool feature of Blogger is the Comment Notification setting. Here you can specify an email address that will be sent a message each time a new comment is added to your blog. You can add your own email address here so that you will be alerted immediately when readers add a comment to an entry, as opposed to having to check back in your past blog entries to see whether any new discussions have started.

Archiving Old Content

Back in the Formatting tab you specified how many posts to display on your blog's home page. As the home page fills up with new posts, eventually old posts will need to be removed from the home page. These older entries can still be accessed, though, because Blogger archives older posts. From the Archiving tab you can specify how often the archiving should occur: daily, weekly, monthly, or not at all (see Figure 6.13) .

SHOULD YOU ALLOW ANYONE TO LEAVE COMMENTS?

Blogger allows you to define who, exactly, can leave comments on your blog: registered Blogger users, anyone, or just those users who are members of your blog. By default, Blogger allows only registered users to leave comments. Many blog owners, however, find this to be restrictive. If you have someone visit your blog who's not a registered user with Blogger but wants to leave a comment, she'll have to take the time to create a Blogger account. Chances are, she'll simply forgo the effort and leave your blog without adding to the discussion.

By allowing anyone to leave comments, visitors who aren't already registered with Blogger won't have the annoyance of having to first create a Blogger account. However, by allowing anyone to leave comments you may find that your blog attracts *comment spammers.* Comment spam is advertising or offensive messages left in the comments of a blog—usually linking back to casino, adult, or pharmaceutical sites—and is an increasing nuisance in the world of blogs. By allowing only registered users, comment spam can be kept to a minimum, because as soon as one account is found to be spamming, it can be disabled. (For example, my blog, www.ScottOnWriting.NET, receives more than 5,000 attempted comment spam messages per year. Thankfully I have filters that automatically reject messages that contain particular keywords common in comment spam.)

Personally, I recommend starting your blog by allowing anyone to leave comments and configuring your blog to email you whenever a new comment is made. If, over time, you find that a number of comment spams are reaching your blog, you may want to either disable comments altogether or allow only registered users to leave comments.

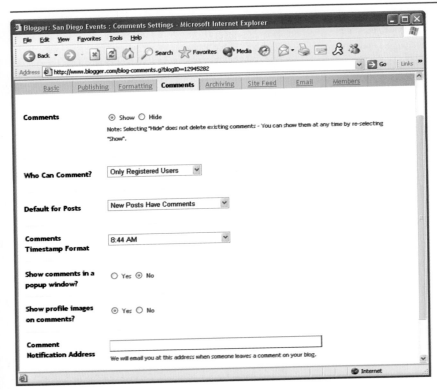

FIGURE 6.12
Use the Comments tab to indicate whether your blog accepts users' comments.

Additionally, you can indicate whether you want each post to have a unique web page. If you set this option to No, a visitor can't view a particular blog entry. Rather, he can only view the home page and the archived pages (which would have all blog entries for a particular day, week, or month, depending on the archiving frequency you specified). However, if you set the Enable Page Posts setting to Yes (the default), each blog entry will have a unique web page. For example, the blog entry I made about the PB Block Party back in the "Adding Content to Your Blog" section, can be viewed directly at http://scottinsandiego.blogspot.com/ 2005/05/pb-block-party.html. By having the blog entry as its own web page, I can easily share a particular blog entry either as a link in a web page or by emailing the web page URL to friends and family.

FIGURE 6.13

Specify the archive frequency from the Archiving tab.

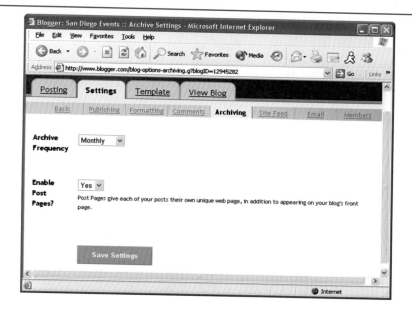

Working with Postings Via Email

In the "Adding Content to Your Blog" section we saw how to use Blogger's WYSIWYG editor to compose a blog entry. In addition to this, Blogger allows you to also post blog content by simply sending an email to a predefined email address. To be able to post via email you'll need to first visit the Email tab (see Figure 6.14) and complete the Mail-to-Blogger Address section, choosing a secret name. After you have chosen this secret name and clicked the Save Settings button, you can then post content to your blog by simply emailing to *username.secretName*@blogger.com. For example, suppose that for my blog I chose the secret name "email"; I could then post content to my blog by simply emailing the content I wanted to appear to scottinsandiego.email@blogger.com.

TIP

Blogger uses the subject of the email as the title for the blog entry, and the body of the email as the blog entry's content. To get the hang of it, after you have configured your blog to accept email posts try sending your blog a few test email messages and observe how various email subjects and bodies affect the content of the post. (Don't worry, you can always delete these test posts through the Posting tab's Edit Posts subtab.)

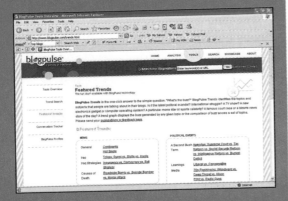

SOMETHING TO TALK ABOUT

What do most people blog about? If you've ever wanted to know how many blogs are out there in cyberspace and what topics are being discussed the most, just visit a site called Blogpulse. With the help of technology such as natural language processing, they are able to study trends in blogging and categorize the most current subjects in sports, news, politics, business, and a few others. You could probably guess that Harry Potter is one of the big entertainment topics; but would you guess that one of the other most popular topics is the seven deadly sins?

Along with posting blog content by email, you can also opt to automatically receive any new blog posts made to a specified email address. If you want to receive an email copy of your posts, provide your email address in the BlogSend Address field.

Republishing Your Blog

As we have seen over the past several sections, Blogger allows you to customize the appearance of your blog through a number of settings. For example, the Formatting tab includes numerous settings that specifically affect the look and feel of the blog's home page. Anytime you edit a setting that dictates the blog's appearance you'll need to republish your blog to have the change take effect.

Republishing your blog is easy and can be done in two ways. First, whenever you change one of your blog's display settings and click the Save Settings button you are prompted with an interface to republish your blog (see Figure 6.15). You can also republish your blog by going to the Posting tab's Status subtab, which provides the same two buttons for republishing shown in Figure 6.15.

When republishing your blog you can republish the *entire* blog or just the blog's index. Republishing the entire blog causes all blog entries to be republished, thereby updating all web pages on your blog with the new settings; republishing the index updates only the blog's home page. I recommend always choosing to republish the entire blog. It can take a bit longer than republishing just the index, but this way you are sure any changes you have made are applied to all pages on the blog.

FIGURE 6.14

Who needs a web browser? Post your blog entries using email!

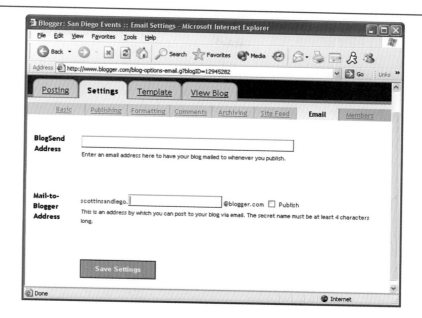

FIGURE 6.15

Republish your entire blog or the index only.

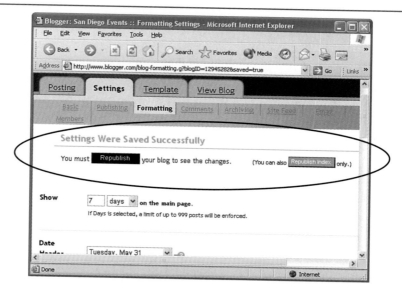

Customizing the Blog's Template

Recall that when creating your blog you were asked to pick a template; for my blog, I chose the Sand Dollar template. The template provides a standardized look and feel for your blog, but you can customize your blog's template or even choose a new template through the Template tab. The Template tab, which is one of the top-level tabs, next to the Settings tab, is shown in Figure 6.16.

The Template tab has two subtabs: Edit Current and Pick New. The Edit Current tab, shown in Figure 6.16, allows you to change the HTML content of your template. As discussed in

Chapter 9, "Bonus Material," web pages are composed of HTML markup. Tools such as Mozilla Composer or Blogger's WYSIWYG editor insulate you from this funky script syntax. Unfortunately, if you want to customize your Blogger template you need to pick through the actual HTML.

This book does not aim to provide a thorough discussion of HTML syntax, although HTML concepts are discussed in more detail in the Bonus Chapter. However, let's take a moment to actually update our template, even though it involves picking through HTML. Specifically, we'll add a link to our blog's site feed.

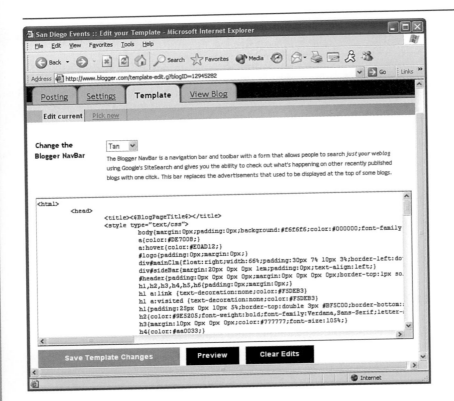

FIGURE 6.16

You can customize the template through the Template tab.

Start by picking through the HTML in the text box until you find the following markup: `<li><a href="http://EDITME!">Edit-Me</a></li>` (this markup is located near the end of HTML content). This is the HTML used to render the links along left-hand side of the Sand Dollar template, the ones that appear under the Links heading (refer to Figure 6.9 for a view of the blog home page).

To preview what the changes will look like, click the Preview button. If the site layout looks funny, return to the Template tab and make sure that you changed the proper markup and did not accidentally delete or move surrounding HTML.

After you have perfected the HTML for your customized template, click the Save Template Changes button. This saves the customizations made to your blog's template; be sure to republish your blog to have the new template changes take effect.

TIP

If you want to replace the template you selected when creating your blog with one of the other premade Blogger templates, simply click the Pick New subtab. This lists the predefined Blogger templates, allowing you to choose a different one than your current template. Do realize, however, that choosing a new template will cause you to lose any customizations made to your existing template.

WHEN BLOGGING BECOMES DANGEROUS

Can you get fired from your company for blogging? Yes, you can. Before you write anything about your job or your company, read this article from a former airline employee. It will make you aware of how companies monitor employee communications. Scary stuff, but a good lesson to learn before you begin writing entries that you intend to be only for the amusement of your friends and family.

Summary

This chapter examined how to create a blog using the free Blogger service. Blogs are an increasingly popular medium for publishing information online and are used by individuals, families, small businesses, and even large corporations as a way to quickly and easily post entries to a website.

Blogs are composed of a series of blog entries. By default, only you, the blog's creator, can add, edit, or delete entries. However, Blogger allows you to optionally invite other individuals to participate in your blog, granting them access to add their own entries. This feature is especially useful for a small business or family blog, where you want to allow the company's employees or the members of the family to all contribute to a single blog.

In addition to making it a cinch to add, edit, and delete blog entries, Blogger provides the standard blog features:

- Visitors can leave comments for a particular blog entry.
- Your blog can provide a site feed for visitors who use aggregator programs.
- You can post to your blog by simply sending an email to a particular, secret email address.

Blogger also makes it easy to customize your blog. There are a bevy of settings you can tweak to tailor your blog to meet your particular needs. If you are familiar with HTML you can even customize your blog's template, meaning that your blog's appearance is totally customizable.

Blogs are a fun and easy way to share your thoughts, views, or knowledge online. Why not get started blogging today?

CHAPTER 7

Sharing Images Online with SnapFish

There will come a time in the not-so-distant future where your children, or perhaps your children's children, will look at you and, with incredulity, stammer, "Pictures used to be stored on *film*? What is this film, and why did it need to be *developed*?" Although we were raised with film-based cameras being the staple at any vacation or family gathering, over the past decade film-based cameras have been going the way of the Dodo bird. Today, it seems, everyone has a digital camera, and why not? Quality, entry-level digital cameras can be had for $100-$200 and come packed with more capacity and features than those more expensive models from years past.

One nice feature of film-based cameras is that after you develop your pictures you have a physical print that you can put in an album. For many years getting a physical print from a digital camera was not a trivial task because only a few up-scale photography stores offered such services. Today, however, virtually all stores that develop film can create prints from digital images. Many also can, for a few dollars extra, provide you with a CD that contains your images. There are even specialized image printers that you can buy that you can use to create prints directly from a digital camera in the comfort of your own home.

Because a digital camera stores its images digitally, these image files can be uploaded to a home computer. From there you can manipulate the images with the appropriate software, resizing them, reducing red-eye, or applying other effects. You can move these images from your computer to your website, email the images directly to friends and family, or use web applications such as SnapFish to share your images online.

In previous chapters you learned how to use the templates included on this book's CD to create your own website, including how to add images to your website. For example, if you recently vacationed in Hawaii and took a slew of pictures with your digital camera, on returning you might want to build a "My Trip to Hawaii" website with various web pages describing your trip and the activities you enjoyed, accompanied by pictures you took on vacation. To create such a site you would use the techniques learned in previous chapters.

What if you didn't want an entire, "My Trip to Hawaii" website, though? What if all you wanted was to share the pictures you took with friends and family, enabling them to order prints of those photos they liked best? A number of free web applications are available that make ordering prints and sharing photos with friends and family a breeze. In this chapter we'll examine one such web application in detail, SnapFish.

"A number of free web applications are available that make ordering prints and sharing photos with friends and family a breeze."

Choosing an Online Image Sharing Service

The first step to sharing your digital photos online is to create an account with a photo sharing service such as SnapFish. SnapFish is just one of a multitude of websites that provide digital image processing and photo sharing.

Other popular image sharing web applications include

► MyPhotoAlbum.com (http://www.myphotoalbum.com/)

► ShutterFly (http://www.shutterfly.com/)

► WebShots (http://www.webshots.com/)

► Flickr (http://www.flickr.com/)

► ImageStation (http://www.imagestation.com/)

All these sites basically have the same core set of features: They make it easy to upload and share your digital images, allowing you and your friends and family to order prints. Although any of these sites would likely meet your needs, I suggest that if you're interested in sharing your photos online you use SnapFish because you can follow along with this chapter.

TIP

In addition to being able to order prints, most of these online photo sharing web applications—including SnapFish—allow you or friends and family to buy photo-related gifts. For example, you can buy Dad a coffee mug with a picture of his grandchildren on it, or a mouse pad with a picture of your family for yourself.

Creating an Account on SnapFish

Before you can upload your digital photos to SnapFish and share them with friends and family you first need to create a free account. Start by firing up your browser and heading over to www.SnapFish.com. On the home page is a link to get you started using SnapFish. Clicking on this takes you to the registration page (shown in Figure 7.1), where you are prompted for your name, email address, and a password.

NOTE

Along with sharing digital photos and ordering prints and photo-related items, SnapFish also will develop film and mail you the prints. If you plan on using this feature you are prompted to provide your mailing address when creating your account.

Congratulations, you now have an account on SnapFish! That was easy. After creating your account you see your customized SnapFish home page, from where you can upload digital photos, order prints, or share your photos with friends and family (see Figure 7.2).

Take a moment to examine the SnapFish home page shown in Figure 7.2. Along the top are four tabs that, when clicked, take you to various pages on the site:

DIGITAL PHOTOGRAPHY REVIEW

This site looks like any other digital photography site—a lot of cameras and peripherals—until you click on the "Learn" menu option. You can learn about infrared photography on your digital camera, fancy filters, and add-on lenses that you work with the flash feature. Maybe you're not quite up to spending more money on gadgets and gizmos to produce exotic photos, but this site does make anyone want to head to the camera store. If your pocketbook is thin, don't worry. They also have techniques that you can try without spending a dime, like creating multiple exposures with your digital camera.

▶ **Home**—When logging on to SnapFish you are taken to this tab, your customized home page. From the home page you can easily accomplish the most common tasks: upload images, order prints, and share photos.

▶ **Photos**—The Photos tab allows you to work with the photos you've already uploaded. You can delete photos from your SnapFish account, organize them into albums, email photos to friends and family, order a photo CD, and so on.

▶ **Store**—After you've uploaded your photos, you may want to order photo-related items, such as a photo book, calendar, coffee mug, or handbag adorned with pictures of your choice. These transactions can be carried out through the Stores tab.

▶ **Account**—From the Account tab you can edit your account settings—name, email address, mailing address, and so on—record commonly used email addresses in an Address Book, and set account-level preferences.

Throughout the remainder of this chapter you'll learn how to use SnapFish to upload and manage your digital pictures, invite friends and family to view your online photo albums, and order prints and gifts.

FIGURE 7.1

To get started, create an account on SnapFish.

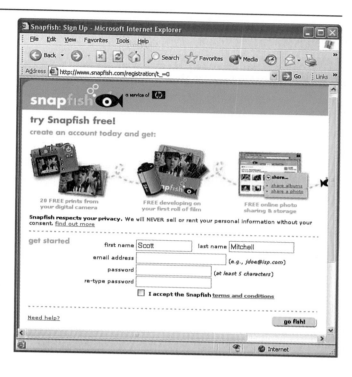

FIGURE 7.2

Welcome to your SnapFish home page.

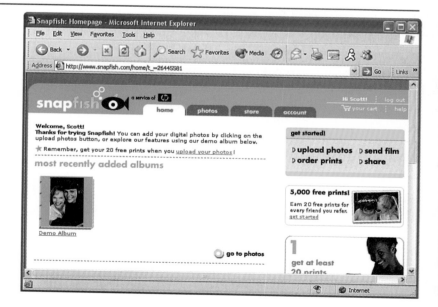

Uploading and Managing Your Digital Pictures

SnapFish organizes your digital pictures using *albums*. An album in SnapFish is similar to a physical picture album: Just like you may have multiple photo albums at home, your SnapFish account may have multiple albums, and each album can hold many pictures. As you'll see shortly, when uploading images to SnapFish you can specify that they be added to an existing album or be placed in a new one. After your images have been added to an album, you can edit the albums through the Photos tab, adding or removing pictures from the album, renaming the album, and so on.

When you created your SnapFish account, a Demo Album was added automatically. This album is a noneditable album—you can't add new images to this album or edit those pictures within. (You can, however, remove the album from your account, which you'll see how to do in the "Edit and Delete Your Pictures and Albums" section.)

The albums in your account are listed in two places: Your SnapFish home page lists the most recently created albums; the Photos tab lists *all* your albums. If you just created your account, your home page should only list one album in the recently created albums section, the Demo Album (refer to Figure 7.2).

To work with the images inside a particular album, simply click the album. This lists the album's images as well as provides a quick list of things you can do. Figure 7.3 shows the screen after I clicked the Demo Album from my home page.

Each of the album's photos is displayed as a small, thumbnail image, but you can click on

the image to see a larger version. The Things You Can Do list on the right provides a list of actions you can take. For example, if you want to add new photos to the currently selected album, simply click the Add Photos link.

> **NOTE**
> You cannot upload images to or edit the pictures in the Demo Album.

Adding Pictures to Your Account

SnapFish provides two ways to add digital pictures to your account. You can upload them directly from your home computer, or you can email them as attachments to save@mysnapfish.com.

> **TIP**
> If you have a camera-enabled, Internet connected mobile phone, you can email pictures taken from your mobile phone directly to your SnapFish account. This involves associating your mobile phone number with your SnapFish account and configuring your phone to email pictures to save@mysnapfish.com. This discussion is beyond the scope of this book, but you can learn more about sending in pictures from your mobile at http://www.snapfish.com/infoemailupload/.

To upload pictures directly from your computer, click the Upload Photos link in the upper right-hand corner. This link is found both on the

Home and Photos tabs. Doing so displays the Upload Photos screen. This screen has two steps. The first step is to choose which album you want the uploaded photos to be saved under. By default, you are prompted to create a new album. If you have existing albums in your account, you can opt to have the photos placed there instead of in a new album. The next step is to select those files you want to upload. Figures 7.4 and 7.5 show these two steps.

To select the files to upload, click the Select Photos button. This displays the file dialog box shown in Figure 7.5 from which you can select the image files from your computer that you want to upload to SnapFish. After you've selected the files to upload from your computer, click OK to initiate the uploading process. Depending on the number and size of your photos and the speed of your Internet connection, this process can take from a few seconds to several minutes. After the files are uploaded you are shown the images you just uploaded.

As mentioned earlier, SnapFish also allows you to email your pictures. This option is useful for sending in pictures from mobile phones or when you are working offline. That is, if you are at your laptop or computer and are not connected to the Internet, you cannot upload your images through the Upload Images web page because you'll be unable to connect to SnapFish. You can, however, create an email message for each image that you want to upload to your account. Granted, these email messages won't get sent until next time you connect to the Internet, but on connecting you won't need to use the SnapFish website to upload your images—they'll be sent directly from your email program.

IDEA GALLERY

http://www.imaging-resource.com/IMCOMP/COMPS01.HTM

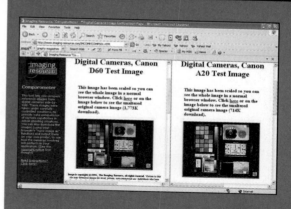

IMAGING RESOURCE

This site displays side-by-side photographs taken by two different cameras for comparison. Their list is extensive and up-to-date; so if you can't choose between the Nikon Coolpix and the Canon Powershot, go to this site and compare them. You can preview images photographed with a flash, snapped indoors and outdoors, and shot in close-up. You can also preview various special camera features that may be the deciding factor when it's time to purchase a new camera.

FIGURE 7.3

Click on an album to view or edit its photos.

FIGURE 7.4

Choose or create the album where your photos will be saved.

FIGURE 7.5
Choose the files you want to upload.

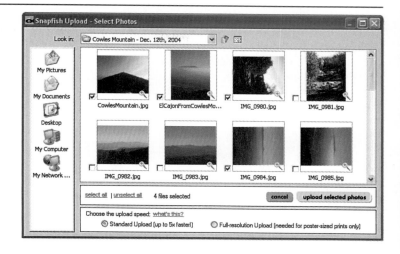

To add pictures to your account through email, simply send an email to save@mysnapfish.com with each image you want to add included as an email attachment. When SnapFish receives this email with your images, it sends an email back to you with a link that, when clicked, allows you to select which of the emailed images you want added to your account, and which ones to discard. Figure 7.6 shows the email SnapFish sent back to me after receiving images I sent to save@snapfish.com.

FIGURE 7.6
When you email save@snapfish.com you'll be sent a confirmation email.

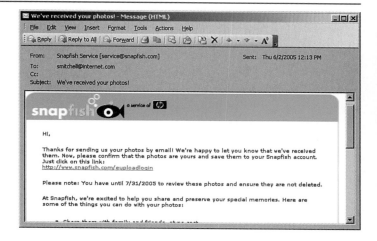

At MyPublisher, you can download free software and use it to lay out attractive photo albums that range from $10–$60. They offer templates from paperback pocketbooks, to more expensive hardcover albums, to deluxe books. Their process is pretty easy. Download the software, upload your photos, edit your photos, and lay out your book with your choice of 80 different templates. Send it off to the company to produce your book. Simple!

"To add pictures to your account through email, simply send an email to save@mysnapfish.com with each image you want to add included as an email attachment."

Edit and Delete Your Pictures and Albums

After uploading pictures to your account, take a moment to review them. To do so, go to the Photos tab, which lists the albums in your account. Click on the album whose pictures you want to review.

Are there pictures that are laid out vertically, but need to be displayed horizontally? Would a particular photo look better with a border around it? Do your images have description captions or is each picture identified with some cryptic caption such as IMG00041? Perhaps of the images you've added, you now realize that there are a couple you don't want in your album.

Fortunately, SnapFish makes editing and deleting pictures as easy as adding them. If you want to edit or delete a single image, first click on the album it exists in and then on the picture itself. In the right-hand column you'll find an assortment of links for editing or deleting the specific image under the Edit & Organize heading (see Figure 7.7).

FIGURE 7.7

The right-hand toolbar lists the links for editing or deleting images.

If you want to edit or delete multiple pictures in an album, click on the album that contains the photos you want to edit or delete. In the right-hand column you'll see a series of links similar to those shown in Figure 7.7. The difference is when you click on these links from the album view you'll be asked to choose what pictures in the album you want to edit or delete.

When viewing an individual photo, the links under the Edit & Organize heading are

- ▶ **Add a Border**—Allows you to choose a border to add to your picture. Realize that adding a border creates a *new*, bordered picture in your album. The original picture, sans the border, remains

untouched. Figure 7.8 shows the Add Borders screen.

- ▶ **Rotate and Flip**—If an image is laid out incorrectly and needs to be flipped, click on this link.

- ▶ **Caption This Photo**—If your pictures have nondescript titles (such as IMG00041), click on this link to provide more intelligible captions.

- ▶ **Move This Photo**—Click this link to move the photo to a different album.

- ▶ **Copy This Photo**—Click this link to send a copy of the picture to a different album.

- ▶ **Delete This Photo**—If you have a photo you want to remove from the album, click this link.

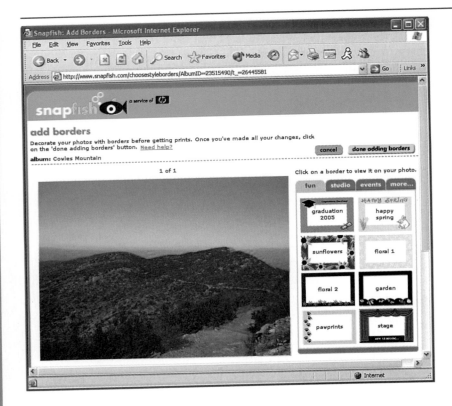

FIGURE 7.8
Add a border to your
pictures.

When viewing all the pictures within a particular album, the options under the Edit & Organize heading include those from the preceding list along with three additional options that allow for editing or deleting the album:

- **Rename Album**—Click this link to rename the selected album.

- **Rearrange**—By default, the order of images within an album is based on the order with which the images were uploaded. You can, however, reorder the images within an album by clicking on the Rearrange link.

- **Remove Album**—If you want to delete an album and all the pictures within, click on this link.

In the next section, you'll learn how to share your pictures and albums with selected friends and families. Following that you'll see how to use SnapFish to order prints and photo-related gifts. Before doing either of these things it would be wise to make sure that your pictures are properly positioned, have germane captions, and belong in appropriately named albums. Using the techniques discussed in this section, you should be able to deftly rotate, add borders, and edit picture captions.

Sharing Your Pictures and Albums with Friends and Family

After you upload pictures to your SnapFish account you can share them with select friends and family. You can share an entire albums or specific pictures. To start sharing your photos, click the Share link from the SnapFish home page or, from the Photos tab, click the Share Albums or Share a Photo link in the Things You Can Do toolbar on the right-hand side of the screen. Additionally, when viewing a particular album or photo there are share links in the toolbar on the right.

If you click the Share link from the home page or choose to share an album, you are taken to a page where you can indicate what albums you want to share (see Figure 7.9). If you clicked on a link to share a particular photo, you are prompted to first choose which album the picture resides in and then select the specific photo (see Figure 7.10).

After you select the albums or photo to share, you are taken to the screen shown in Figure 7.11, where you can enter the email addresses of the friends and family you want to share your pictures with. For each email address you provide, that person will receive an email from SnapFish inviting him to view the albums or picture you have shared. You can customize the email your friends and family will receive through the Subject and Message text boxes.

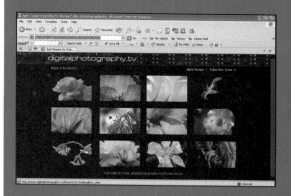

DIGITALPHOTOGRAPHY.TV

Sign up for the cool newsletter, or check out the inspirational photo gallery at this site. Even if you're not an expert photographer, you'll be able to draw inspiration and ideas from this photographer's website (including closeups of flowers, a trip to Yosemite, and links to other art photography sites on the Web).

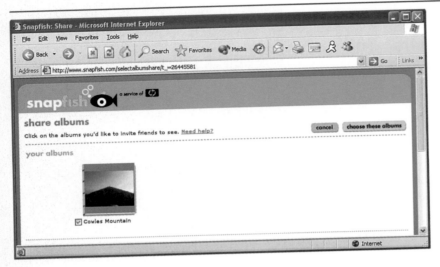

FIGURE 7.9
If you decide to share an
album, you can choose
which albums to share.

FIGURE 7.10
When sharing a photo,
you must select a single
photograph to share.

FIGURE 7.11

Provide the email addresses of those with whom you want to share your pictures.

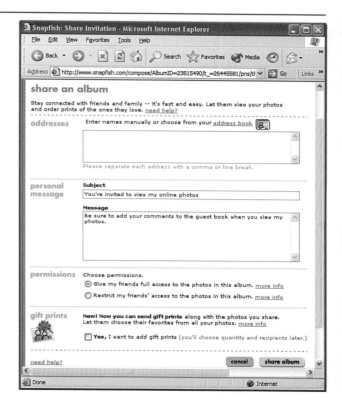

SnapFish offers an *address book* feature to quickly add email addresses of friends and family. To add email addresses of friends and family in the address book, click on the Address Book link above the Addresses text box in Figure 7.11.

Whenever you share pictures with a person, they are automatically added to the address book. You can also manually add or remove friends and family from your address book by going to the Account tab and clicking on the Edit Address Book link.

If you opt to share an album you need to choose whether you want to give your friends and family full access to the photos in the album, or limit them to just viewing the photo album. If you give your friends and family full access to the album, they can order prints and gifts or copy your albums' pictures to their SnapFish account. (Don't worry, granting full access doesn't allow friends and family to delete your albums' photos.) If you don't want to allow your friends and family to copy your albums' photos to their account or order prints or gifts, choose to limit them to just viewing the pictures by selecting the Restrict My

FLICKR

Flickr is something lots of people have started using because they offer so many features for sharing photos, organizing albums, and posting to blogs. Best of all, a basic account is free. Lots of sites offer free photo storage and sharing, but check out Flickr if you want something a little more robust. When people come to view your photos, they can leave comments and tags on the pictures. You can also create group-photo pools so that if a bunch of people have photos from the same event, everyone can upload to the same place.

Friends' Access to These Photos in This Album option.

You can also include gift prints for each person you're sharing your photos with. By adding gift prints you are offering to buy a specified number of prints for the recipient viewing your shared pictures. When adding gift prints you can specify how many gift prints to give to each recipient and will be charged based on the total number of gift prints you include. (At the time of this writing, 4"x6" gift prints cost $0.12 each with a minimal shipping and handling charge related to the total number of prints issued per recipient.)

> ### "You can also include gift prints for each person you're sharing your photos with."

After you have specified the email addresses of the friends and family you want to share your albums or photos with, customized the subject and message, and set the permissions and gift print options, finish by clicking the Share Album link at the bottom of the page. This sends out an email to the recipients you have specified inviting them to view your album. Figure 7.12 shows the email invitation sent to those recipients you decided to share your pictures with.

FIGURE 7.12
Your friends and family will receive an email invitation to view your pictures.

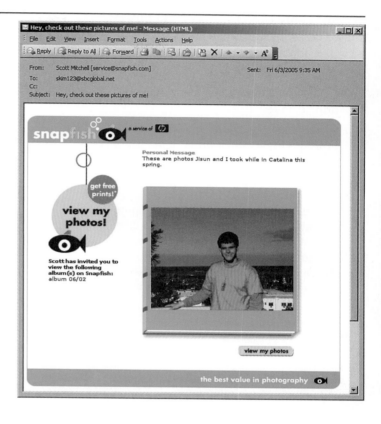

Ordering Prints and Gifts

Although being able to view pictures online is a neat feature, there's no substitute for a print. A print can be put in a picture book, hung up in a cubicle at work, or slapped up on the refrigerator. SnapFish makes it easy to order prints from the digital images in your account. Simply select those images you want prints for, pay for each print (along with a nominal shipping and handling charge), and within a few days you'll receive prints of those pictures in the mail. And not only can you order prints for yourself, but your friends and family also can order prints from albums or pictures you share.

To order prints, click the Order Prints link in the home page or from the Photos tab. When ordering prints, proceed through the following steps:

1. Select which digital pictures you want printed.

2. Specify the dimensions, quantities, and print quality for each print. SnapFish offers a variety of print dimensions: wallet sets, 4x6, 5x7, 8x10, 11x14, and additional poster print sizes (see Figure 7.13).

3. Provide payment information, shipping options, and the shipping address. Like virtually all online stores, PayPal accepts all major credit cards and offers various shipping speeds, from standard speed (3-5 business days) to overnight delivery.

When choosing the pictures to receive prints for you may notice that certain images in your album have a little orange triangle next to them. Similarly, when selecting the print dimensions, you may find that certain print dimensions for certain pictures have an orange triangle next to them (see Figure 7.13). This orange triangle warns that the digital image's resolution is too low for the specified print dimension. SnapFish still lets you order prints where this warning applies, but the quality of the print may be low.

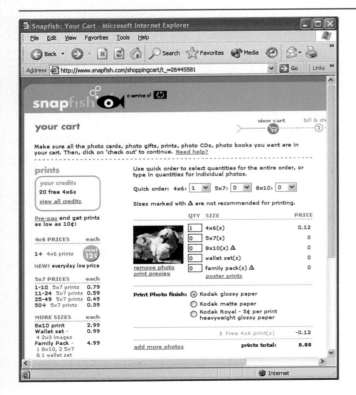

FIGURE 7.13

If an image's resolution is too low, you'll see an orange triangle.

> **NOTE**
>
> A digital picture's resolution depends on the digital camera's settings and whether you've modified the file prior to uploading it to SnapFish (such as resizing the image to smaller dimensions). Most modern digital cameras, when taken with the high resolution, provide image files that can be printed on any print size. Consult your digital camera's documentation on how to set the image resolution.

In addition to being able to order prints, SnapFish also sells various gifts that can have your pictures imprinted on them. By clicking on the Store tab you are taken to the SnapFish store, which lists all photo-related items for sale (see Figure 7.14). You can order photo books, mugs, calendars, t-shirts, mouse pads, handbags, and other assorted gifts that come preprinted with a select image from your albums. The prices and shipping and handling for these gifts vary, so be sure to check out the SnapFish store for more details.

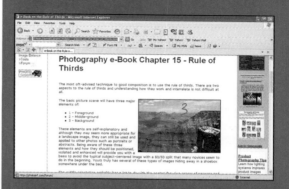

PHOTO COMPOSITION ARTICLES

This site is a wonderful resource for learning how to create a picture. No matter what kind of camera you have, taking attractive photos takes skill in composition and direction in art. This great little site tells you how to use the "Rule of Thirds" to create the perfect photo, follow color rules, and frame your picture while shooting. Some of the tips are pretty simple once you read them, but not always obvious to the beginning photographer. You'll be amazed by how much you learn from this site.

FIGURE 7.14
Have your photos imprinted on mugs, calendars, towels, and more!

Summary

If you have digital images that you want to share with friends and family, you have a number of options: You can simply email those friends and family your images; you can build a family/personal website, as discussed in Chapter 3, "Creating a Family/Personal Website," adding the assorted images to web pages on your site; or you can use a service such as SnapFish to upload your images and share them with select friends and family.

Each of these approaches has its advantages and disadvantages. If you want to share your pictures with a specific group of people, you should either email your pictures to those people or use a service such as SnapFish. The advantage of SnapFish is that those who are invited to view your photos can order prints and gifts, which is not possible when emailing pictures. If, however, you want to let anyone view your pictures, you'll want to create a public website, as discussed in earlier chapters.

As you saw in this chapter, SnapFish makes sharing pictures with friends and family incredibly easy. Simply upload the images you want to share and then send out an invitation to friends and family. It's that easy! After you've uploaded your photos, those you've invited to view your pictures can order prints or photo-related gifts, such as calendars, coffee mugs, and mouse pads. Services such as SnapFish show the future of personal photography. There will be a day—and it's not far away—when a child will look at you dumbfounded when you mention the words *camera* and *film* in the same sentence.

CHAPTER 8

Hanging Out and Making Friends at MySpace

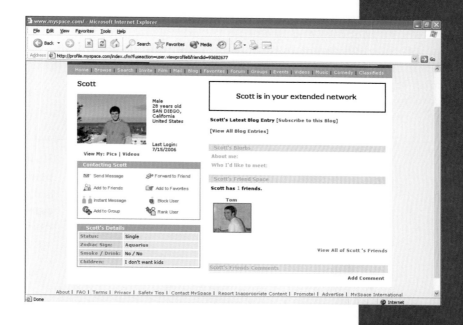

In the 1960s, psychologist Stanley Milgram hypothesized that while there may be billions of people, everyone on Earth can be connected through a relatively short series of social acquaintances. Surprisingly, his experiments found that people in the United States are connected, on average, by just six degrees of separation. In other words, although I have never met Angelina Jolie, perhaps I know someone who has a friend who is a coworker of someone who's a relative of Angelina's hair stylist! This collection of acquaintances—your friends, your friends' friends, their friends, and so on—makes up your *social network*, and is a great place to make new friends (see Figure 8.1).

Before the emergence of the World Wide Web, social networks grew rather slowly. Maybe you met some of your friend's pals at a party, or met your sibling's friends when visiting, but expanding your social network typically required planned meetings and in-person introductions. Today, however, making new friends through your social network is as easy as going online to any number of "social networking" sites, creating an account, and adding your friends to your network. With your new network, you can start making new friends by chatting and sharing pictures with your friend's friends.

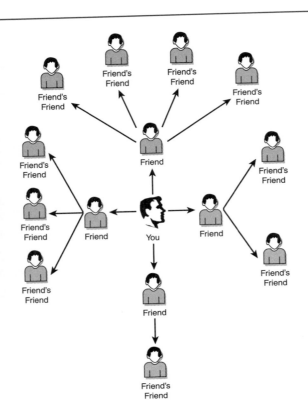

FIGURE 8.1

Your social network is made up of your friends, your friends' friends, their friends, and so on.

There are many social networking websites. Most are free and allow anyone to join, while some are more exclusive or charge a membership fee. The most popular social networking site, by far, is MySpace. A study by Hitwise in July 2006 reported that MySpace was the Internet's most visited site, surpassing search giants Yahoo! and Google. MySpace boasts over 95 million registered users and 1.5 billion page views *per day*.

Along with its social networking features, MySpace also makes it easy for its users to express themselves through personalized profile pages, video and picture sharing, blogs, and other features. This chapter shows you how to use MySpace to stay in touch with old friends and meet new and interesting people through your social network.

> *"MySpace boasts over 95 million registered users and 1.5 billion page views per day."*

Joining MySpace

Getting started on MySpace is free and easy. Fire up your web browser, surf over to www.MySpace.com, and click the Sign Up link from the home page to join the MySpace community. The sign up process creates your profile and is broken down into three steps. In the first step, shown in Figure 8.2, you supply your general, account-related information, such as your email address, name, and password. After entering the requested information, click "Sign Up" to proceed to the second step.

MODMYSPACE

While your MySpace profile's background and colors can be personalized, such customizations must be specified in Hypertext Markup Language, or HTML, the markup language of web pages. Tailoring your profile's appearance can be time consuming and frustrating if you don't have any experience or interest in learning HTML. If you fall within that camp, check out ModMySpace. Simply provide the background and colors you want for your profile through a series of drop-down lists and textboxes, and ModMySpace automatically creates the HTML to insert into your profile!

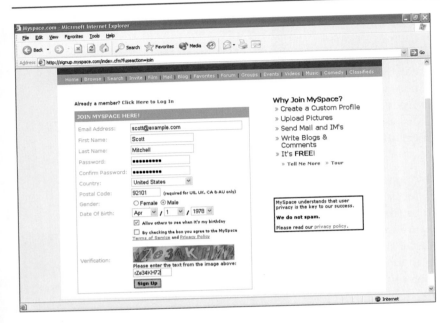

FIGURE 8.2
Sign up to get started with MySpace.

Next, you can optionally associate a picture with your profile. If you don't want to upload a picture, you can click the "Skip for now" link to bypass this step.

TIP

If you currently don't have a picture you want to associate with your profile, don't worry! You can always add a picture later.

To get your social network started, invite your friends to join MySpace. You can invite as many or as few friends as you want. After your friends join, they are automatically added to your social network.

Congratulations, you are now part of the MySpace community!

FIGURE 8.3
Include a picture with your profile.

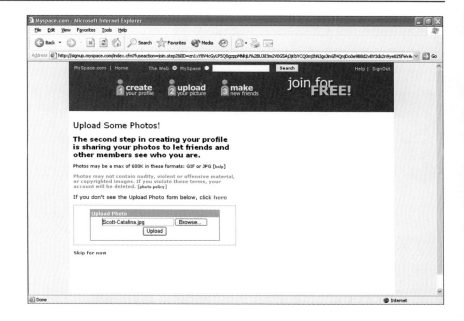

FIGURE 8.4
Broaden your social network by inviting your friends to MySpace.

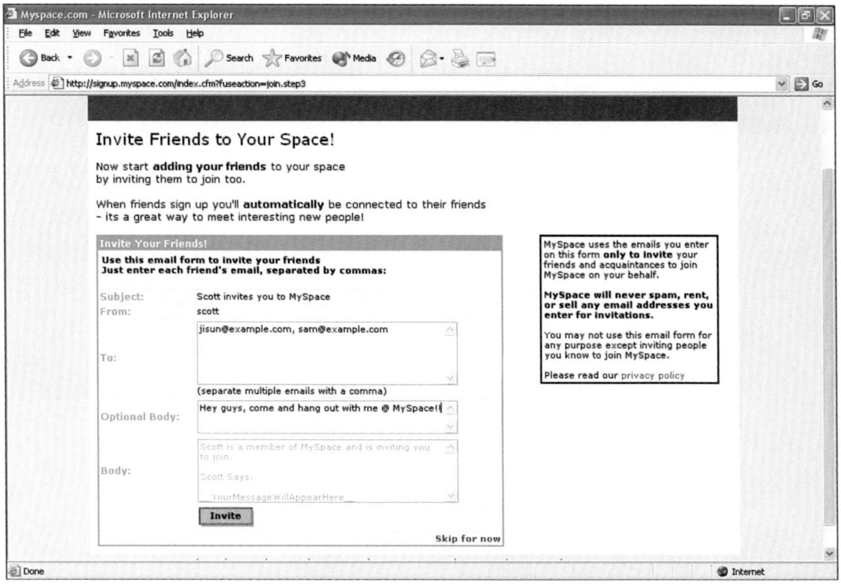

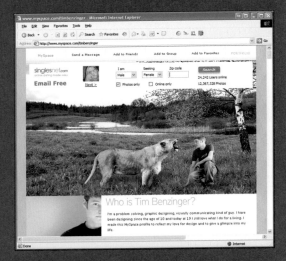

LEARN FROM THE BEST

Professional-looking, highly-customized MySpace profiles are possible! Just check out graphic designer Tim Benzinger's profile. If you're comfortable with HTML, go to your browser's View menu and choose the Source option. This option shows you the entire HTML for Tim's profile. Search for <style> to find Tim's HTML modifications. If HTML is not your thing, drop Tim a line—perhaps he'll share his secrets!

When you log in to MySpace or click the Home link at the top of any page on MySpace, you are taken to your account page (see Figure 8.5). There you can update your profile, change your account settings, upload photos, manage your blog, and much more. In addition to your account page, you also have a profile page where friends can view your profile, leave a comment, and read your blog (see Figure 8.6). To view your profile page, click the "View My Profile" link on your account page.

The remainder of this chapter explores ways to customize your profile page, upload and share photos, and build your social network.

TIP

On your account page, you'll find a box labeled, "Tell people about your MySpace," which provides the URLs to your MySpace profile and blog. Your profile's URL will look like www.MySpace.com/*AccountNumber*. *AccountNumber* is a large number (such as 963146654). You can point your friends and family to your MySpace profile by sending them this URL.

To make your profile's URL more memorable, you can create a MySpace User Name, so that your profile can be accessed using a URL such as www.MySpace.com/*ScottsHomePage*. See "Configuring Your Name Information" for more information.

FIGURE 8.5

Manage your profile, blog, photos, and more from your account page.

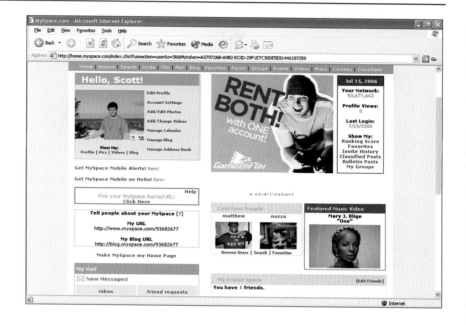

FIGURE 8.6

All MySpace users can view your profile page.

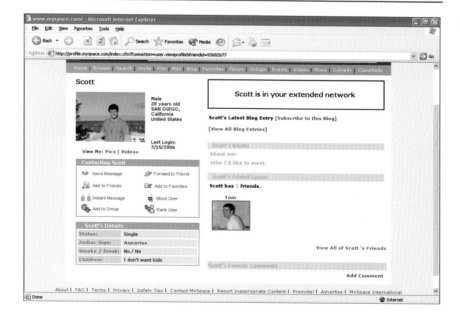

Expanding Your Profile

Your profile can include all sorts of information—your interests, your hobbies, your hometown, your favorite movies and TV shows, the schools you've attended, the companies you've worked for, and other related information. When you sign up, MySpace collects only the information necessary to join the MySpace community. To expand your profile, click the "Edit Profile" link from your account page.

The Profile Edit page is broken down into various sections—Interests & Personality, Name, Basic Info, Background & Lifestyle, and so on—with each section having its own set of questions. In the Basic Info section, for example, you can share your gender, birth date, occupation, location, and ethnicity. You can fill out as many or as few of the questions as you like. To jump to a particular section, simply click the section name in the list of links along the top of the page (see Figure 8.7).

Take a moment to flesh out your profile. For now, just answer the questions in the Interests & Personality, Basic Info, and Background & Lifestyle sections. Next, click the "View My Profile" link in the upper right corner of the Profile Edit page. This takes you to your public profile page. As Figure 8.8 shows, the values entered for your profile are displayed here.

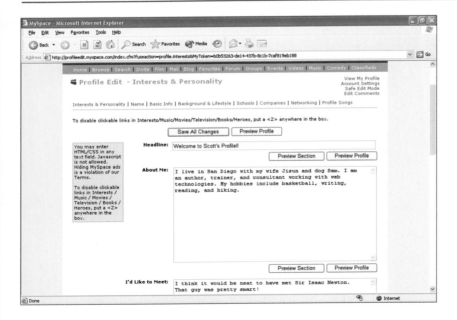

FIGURE 8.7

Update and expand your profile.

FIGURE 8.8

Update and expand your profile.

Customizing Your Profile Page's Layout and Colors

By default, all MySpace profile pages have the same layout—black text on a white background with light gray borders (see Figure 8.8). However, if you view other MySpace users' profile pages, you'll quickly find that many people have customized their profiles with different backgrounds, fonts, and colors. Unfortunately, personalizing your profile page is not as easy as selecting colors and backgrounds from a drop-down list. Instead, you must enter the appropriate *Hypertext Markup Language (HTML)* in the textboxes within the Interests & Personality section in the Profile Edit page.

To customize your profile page so that it displays a yellow background with red borders,

go to the Profile Edit page and, in the About Me textbox, add the following markup:

```
<style>
  body { background-color: red; }
  table, tr, td { background-color: yellow; }
</style>
```

> **NOTE**
>
> A web page defines how it is to be displayed using *Hypertext Markup Language,* or HTML. HTML defines how content should be displayed in a web page and is used to customize your profile page's appearance. Chapter 9, "Bonus Material," provides a more thorough discussion of HTML and its uses.

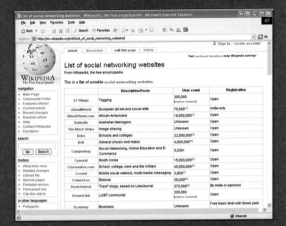

FIND OTHER SOCIAL NETWORKING WEBSITES

MySpace is but one website in a sea of social networking websites. Other popular social networking websites include Facebook, Classmates.com, Friendster, Reunion.com, and Xanga. Each social networking site offers a different approach to the concept. Some are free, others charge a membership fee. Some are open to all, others are more choosey about who can join. To review a comprehensive list of social networking sites and their focus, user count, and registration criteria, check out the list of social networking sites available at Wikipedia.

Next, click the "Save All Changes" button at the top of the Profile Edit page and click the "View My Profile" link to view your modified profile. As Figure 8.9 shows, the yellow background with red borders is a bit hard on the eyes, but it highlights the personalization possibilities.

TIP

For help with customizing your MySpace profile page, you can post your questions at the MySpace Customizing Forum. Simply click the Forum link at the top of any page, open the MySpace Customizing Forum, and post your questions! As the MySpace Frequently Asked Questions page says, "If you do not know HTML, you can reach out and make a new friend by asking someone who has color, graphics, and/or sound on their Profile page how they did it. People on MySpace are friendly and always willing to help, so just ask! This is a great way to meet new people!"

There are also many websites that provide tutorials and step-by-step guides for customizing your profile page. Just head over to your favorite search engine and search on keywords "MySpace," "HTML," and "profile."

Configuring Your Name Information

Your profile page is available online at www.MySpace.com/*AccountNumber*. *AccountNumber* is a large number, such as 963146654. Such a URL is hard for you and your friends and family to remember. Thankfully, MySpace allows you to create a MySpace User Name, which is a name or phrase associated with your profile page.

FIGURE 8.9

The profile page now has a yellow background with red borders.

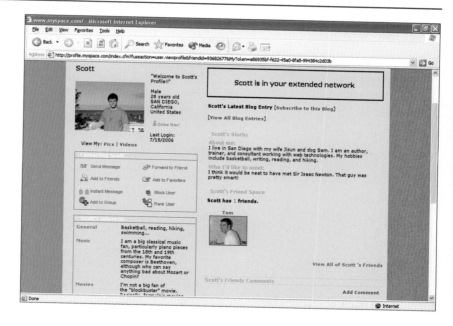

After you've established your MySpace User Name, your profile page can be visited at www.MySpace.com/*UserName*.

In addition to a User Name, your MySpace account also contains a Display Name. The Display Name is shown on your profile page. Your User Name is not shown anywhere, but rather is solely used as a shortcut to your profile page (www.MySpace.com/*UserName*). You can change your Display Name as often as you want, but your User Name can only be set once and it is *permanent*.

To create a User Name, go to the Profile Edit page and browse to the Name section. The Name section allows you to change your Display Name, First Name, and Last Name settings, and also lets you create your User Name, if you've not done so already (see Figure 8.10).

*"You can change your Display Name as often as you want, but your User Name can only be set once and it is **permanent**."*

To create a User Name, click on the "Pick your MySpace User Name/URL" link. This link takes you to a page where you can select your User Name. After you've picked a User Name, your profile can be reached at either www.MySpace.com/*UserName* or www.MySpace.com/*AccountNumber*.

NOTE

Each MySpace member's User Name must be unique. With over 95 million users, chances are your first choice for User Name has already been taken. To help maximize the chances of finding an available User Name, try adding numbers, such as Scott_92101.

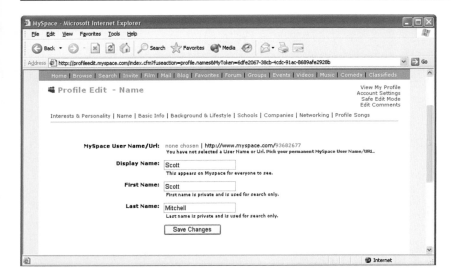

FIGURE 8.10
Manage your Display Name and User Name settings.

Creating a Blog and Sharing Your Pictures

The previous two chapters examined how to create a blog using Blogger and how to create and share digital pictures using SnapFish. If you want a professional-level blog with all the bells and whistles, or you want to allow friends and family to order prints and other memorabilia from your online photos, then Blogger and SnapFish are excellent choices. If, however, you only need simple blog and photo sharing capabilities, MySpace can provide you with these services.

Uploading and Sharing Your Photos

To start sharing photos, click on the "Add/Edit Photos" link from your account page. To add a new picture, start by clicking the Browse button and selecting a picture from your computer to

upload. After you've picked a picture to upload, click the Upload button. That's all there is to it!

Your uploaded photos are listed at the bottom of the page. Each image can have a caption added to it or be deleted entirely from the system. The first photo in your album is considered your default photo. This image is shown on your profile and when you make comments in your friends' profiles. To select a different picture as the default photo, click the picture's "Set as default" buttons (see Figure 8.12).

You may pick one picture to be "ranked" by your fellow MySpace community members. To nominate a picture for ranking, click the picture's "Add to Ranking" button. When another MySpace user visits your profile, he can click the "Rank User" link to rank your selected picture, giving it a ranking from 1 to 10.

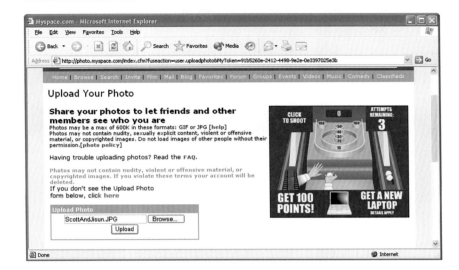

FIGURE 8.11

Add your favorite photos to MySpace.

FIGURE 8.12

Manage your uploaded pictures.

A SITE DEDICATED TO RATING PHOTOS

MySpace allows its users to optionally nominate one of their pictures to be rated on a scale of 1 to 10 by other MySpace members. If you get a kick out of rating others or want a larger audience to rate your picture, check out HOT or NOT, the original picture rating website.

TIP

By default, your photos can be viewed by all MySpace members. To make your photo album private (meaning it can only be viewed by you), scroll down until you reach the "Allow your photos to be viewable by" section and choose the "Only You" option.

After you've added your pictures, visitors to your profile can click the "View My Pics" link to explore your album. While any registered user can view your photos (assuming you've not made your album private), only friends can leave a comment. In "Growing Your Social Network," we'll discuss how to add friends to your network.

NOTE

In addition to photos, MySpace allows you to upload and share videos. To start sharing your videos, click the "Add/Change Videos" link from your account page.

Expressing Yourself with Your Blog

Your blog is like an online journal—a place to keep friends and family up to date with the latest news. To start blogging, click the "Manage Blog" link from your account page. This takes you to the Blog Control Center where you can

▶ Post a new blog entry.

▶ Customize your blog's appearance.

▶ Examine which other MySpace readers have *subscribed* to your blog.

▶ View the latest posts from the blogs to which you've subscribed.

To make your first blog entry, click the "Post New Blog" link. This link takes you to the Post a New Blog Entry page where you can enter content for your blog entry (see Figure 8.13).

All blog entries require a subject and a body. When viewing your profile, users see the subjects of your most recent blog entries; clicking on the subject displays the blog's body. When entering the blog's body, you can use the formatting controls to change the text color or style and to insert smileys, links, and images.

By default, other MySpace members can add comments to your blog entries. If you want to prevent this, click the "disable Kudos &

comments" checkbox. Note the four Privacy options that determine who can read your blog entry:

▶ Public—*everyone* can read your blog entries

▶ Diary—only you can read your blog entries

▶ Friends—limit access to your MySpace friends; we'll discuss how to add friends to your network in the "Growing Your Social Network" section

▶ Preferred List—from the Blog Control Center, you can maintain a "Preferred List" of MySpace users; this option limits access to the blog entry to only those specifically noted in this list

To post your blog entry, click the "Preview & Post" button.

FIGURE 8.13
Add a new entry to your blog.

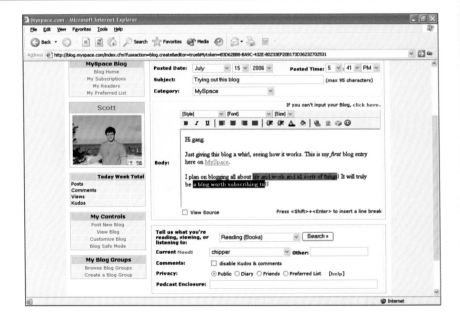

After you've established your blog, your profile page will list the subjects of your most recent blog entries. Visitors can read one of your blog entries by clicking on the subject from your profile page or by visiting your blog page directly at blog.MySpace.com/*AccountNumber* (or blog.MySpace.com/*UserName*, if you've created a User Name).

To edit or remove a blog entry, go to your blog web page and click the Edit or Remove links (see Figure 8.14).

If you check out another MySpace member's blog, you'll find a subscribe link at the top of the page. From your Blog Control Center, click on "My Subscriptions" to view the most recent blog entries from the list of blogs to which you've subscribed. To see which users have subscribed to your blog, click the "My Readers" link.

> **TIP**
>
> Unlike your profile, you don't have to be an HTML mastermind to personalize your blog's background and colors. From your Blog Control Center, click the "Customize Blog" link to choose display options for your blog page.

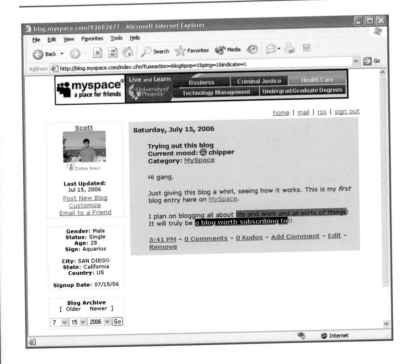

FIGURE 8.14
Your blog page lists your most recent blog entries.

Growing Your Social Network

At MySpace, your social network is made up of *friends*. There are various ways to add friends to your network. Recall that when you first joined MySpace, you could invite friends to also join MySpace (see Figure 8.4). If those invitees join MySpace, they automatically become your friends. You can ask others to become your friends by visiting their profiles and clicking the "Add to Friends" link. This action sends a message to the user asking her whether she wants to become your friend. If she accepts, you'll have added a new friend to your network! Conversely, you may receive messages from other MySpace users who have found your profile and would like to become friends.

Even if you didn't invite anyone when registering, and even if you haven't requested to add users as your friends, you already have one friend. Tom, the creator of MySpace, is automatically added as a friend to every new MySpace member's account. He's a popular guy!

Your friends are listed on your account page. If you have many friends, your account page will only list the first few. To view *all* of your friends, click the "View All of My Friends" link. You can also see which friends have birthdays this week by clicking the "View Upcoming Birthdays" link. To remove friends from your list, click the "Edit Friends" link, select the friends you want to remove from your network, and click the "Delete Selected Friends" button.

> **TIP**
>
> You can send messages to MySpace users, send a mass email to all of your friends, and manage friend requests through the "My Mail" section on your account page.

FIGURE 8.15

View and manage your friends list.

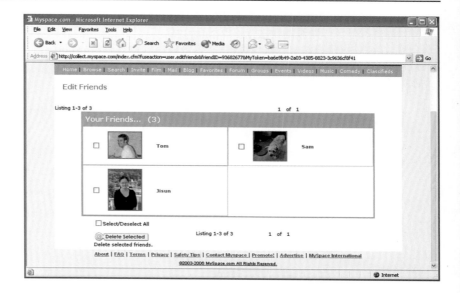

IN A BAND? PUBLICIZE YOURSELF ON MYSPACE!

MySpace offers free band profiles and will host up to four original songs in MP3 format. Up and coming bands can use MySpace to reach a potential audience of millions. Moreover, having an online presence enables bands to communicate with and stay rooted to their fan base. If your band's music is well-received by the MySpace community, the sky's the limit! Just ask indie band Hollywood Undead, a California band that, only weeks after publishing their tracks on MySpace, saw over 10,000 downloads *per day*!

Making New Friends

MySpace makes it easy to meet new people. The concept of social networking sites is that your friends' friends are likely to be people who share similar interests, hobbies, and personalities with you, and therefore make good candidates for new friends. When viewing a friend's profile, you can see his list of friends. Clicking on one of your friends' friends takes you to his profile page, where you can learn about him. If you'd like to get to know him better, you can drop him a line by clicking on the "Send Message" link or by adding him to your friends network.

> *"The concept of social networking sites is that your friends' friends are likely to be people who share similar interests, hobbies, and personalities with you, and therefore make good candidates for new friends."*

MySpace also includes a powerful search mechanism for finding people with similar interests and digging up long-lost friends and classmates. From any MySpace page, click the Search link at the top.

The search page, shown in Figure 8.16, offers four search modes:

- ▶ Search MySpace Profiles
- ▶ Find a Friend
- ▶ Find Your Classmates
- ▶ Affiliations for Networking

FIGURE 8.16
Find friends and class-mates, past or present, with MySpace Search.

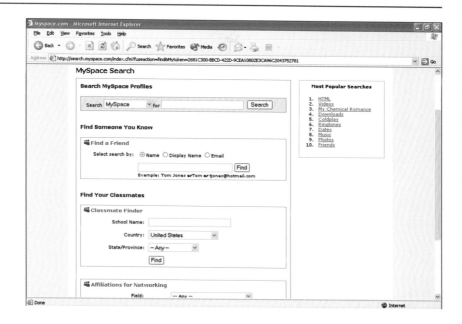

The Search MySpace Profiles option is useful for finding potential friends who share similar interests. From the search drop-down list you can choose whether to search all of MySpace, just the blogs, or particular profile sections, such as General Interest, Music Interest, Movies Interest, and so on.

If you are looking for a particular MySpace user or are curious if an old friend might also be a member of MySpace, use the Find a Friend search option. Here you can search for a user by her real name, her display name, or her email address.

Another great way to find old friends is to use the Classmate Finder option. Start by entering the school name to search for along with the country and state or province. MySpace will then list any matching schools in that region. If you see your old school there, click on it to see a list of MySpace users who have also

attended that school. You can further narrow the search results by gender, age range, major or minor, status as a current student or an alum, graduation year or years attended, and other parameters.

TIP

Want to let old or current classmates find you through the Classmate Finder search? If so, make sure you specify the schools you attended in your profile. From the Profile Edit page, click on the Schools section to specify which schools you've attended or are attending as well as major, minor, graduation date, and other related information.

If you've joined MySpace for networking with peers in your business or avocation, use the Affiliations for Networking search to easily find others on MySpace who are also interested in

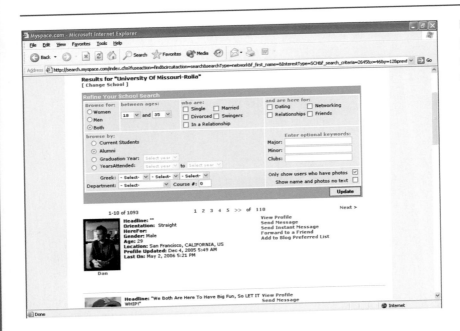

FIGURE 8.17

Find fellow alums or classmates who are also on MySpace.

networking. Choose the field, sub-field, and role of interest—such as Nightlife, Marketing, and Promoter—along with any keywords and click Find to search for others interested in networking in the same area.

If you are interested in networking, be sure to specify your networking categories through your profile. From the Profile Edit page, go to the Networking section. There you can choose any number of fields, sub-fields, and roles that interest you, along with any description.

Summary

Social networking websites such as MySpace offer a degree of interconnectedness not possible before the advent of the Internet. With a few clicks of the mouse, you can add your latest vacation photos to your MySpace site, send a message to all of your friends, blog about your new cat, and make new friends from around the world who share similar interests and hobbies.

As we saw in this chapter, getting started with MySpace is free and easy. After you've created an account, you can manage a blog, upload and share pictures or video, grow your social network, send emails to other MySpace users, and search for long-lost friends or past classmates. In addition to these features, there are many more offerings, including calendars, address books, forums, groups, and events, along with an entire section dedicated to music and music videos from both well-known and independent artists.

MySpace is a fun place to hang out, to keep in touch with old friends, and to make new ones. With its large user base, chances are many people you know are already members at MySpace. So, go ahead and give MySpace a try!

CHAPTER 9

Bonus Material

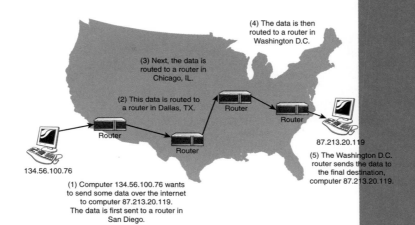

(4) The data is then routed to a router in Washington D.C.

(3) Next, the data is routed to a router in Chicago, IL.

(2) This data is routed to a router in Dallas, TX.

Router

Router

Router

Router

134.56.100.76

87.213.20.119

(1) Computer 134.56.100.76 wants to send some data over the internet to computer 87.213.20.119. The data is first sent to a router in San Diego.

(5) The Washington D.C. router sends the data to the final destination, computer 87.213.20.119.

When writing this book I wanted to focus on the task at hand: showing how to easily create your own websites by customizing provided templates using Mozilla Composer. There were some peripheral topics that I wanted to include, but felt that their inclusion into the book's text detracted from its main purpose. Instead, these tangents are instead presented here, as bonus material on the CD.

The bonus material contains three sections:

- **HTML—The Language of Web Pages**—While Composer makes creating and editing web pages as simple as editing or creating a document with a word processor, underneath the covers Composer is generating appropriate *HTML*. HTML is the markup language used to create web pages. This section, which was initially in Chapter 2, "Creating a Website," provides a discussion on what HTML is and its purpose.

- **Understanding How the Internet Works**—To visit a website, all you have to do is enter the site's name into your browser's Address window. But how does your computer, based on a website name alone, know how to get the specified web page from the appropriate web server? This section, which was initially in Chapter 2, examines how Internet-connected computers are addressed and how special computers called *DNS servers* act as a phone book on the Internet, tying domain names to web server addresses.

- **Optimizing Your Digital Pictures**—Many digital cameras take high-resolution photographs that are oftentimes far too large in both dimensions and file size. After taking images from a digital camera, you'll likely want to resize the images to a smaller dimension. This section discusses some important digital picture terminology and shows how to resize those large image files.

As with the book, if you have any comments or questions regarding the bonus material, please don't hesitate to drop me an email at mitchell@4GuysFromRolla.com.

HTML—The Language of Web Pages

Whenever you navigate to a web page through a web browser, the browser requests the page from the appropriate web server and displays the retrieved page. Recall that the web page itself is nothing more than a file on the web server. The file's contents describe how the page should be displayed in the browser.

"A web page defines how it is to be displayed using a markup language called Hypertext Markup Language, or HTML."

Specifically, a web page defines how it is to be displayed using a markup language called *Hypertext Markup Language*, or *HTML*. HTML defines how content should be displayed in a web page. It uses *tags* to indicate formatting. For example, the *bold tag*, denoted <b>, indicates that its inner text should be displayed in a bold font. The *italic tag*, <i>, indicates that its inner text should be displayed in italics. Given the following HTML markup in a web page, Figure 9.1 shows what would be displayed in a web browser.

```
This is <b>bold</b>
while this is <i>italic</i>.
This, you'll see, is both <b><i>bold and
italic</i></b>.
```

The important thing to realize is that every web page you visit with your browser is composed of HTML markup. It is this markup that describes how to display the web page in your browser.

When you visit a web page through a web browser, you can view the web page's HTML markup. In Internet Explorer, go to the View menu and then choose the Source option; in the Mozilla browser, click on the View menu and choose the Page Source menu option. This will display the web page's HTML content. To fully appreciate how complex this HTML markup can become, take a moment to visit Ford's website at www.ford.com. This website, shown in Figure 9.2, is fairly simple looking, but the HTML required to display this page is daunting. Listing 9.1 lists only a portion of the HTML markup for Ford's homepage.

FIGURE 9.1

HTML specifies how content should be formatted.

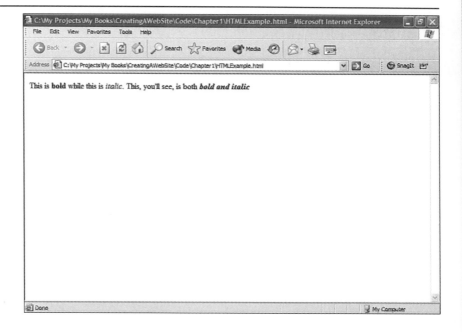

CHAPTER 9   BONUS MATERIAL

LISTING 9.1   A Portion of the HTML Markup for Ford's Homepage

```
    <BODY bgcolor="#FFFFFF" text="#666666"
link="#CC6600" alink="#CC6600"
    vlink="#CC6600" topmargin="0"
leftmargin="0"
    marginwidth="0" marginheight="0">
<!-- Inserted by Content Management Server:
BEGIN EmbedBodyBeginHook -->

<!-- Inserted by Content Management Server:
END EmbedBodyBeginHook -->

    <DIV id="undecided">
        <TABLE border="0" cellpadding="0"
cellspacing="0" width="200"  >
            <TR>
                <TD class="greyHome"
valign="top">
<A
href="/en/vehicles/vehicleShowroom/default.
htm?referrer=home">
Browse all our brands</A> 
<A
href="/en/vehicles/vehicleShowroom/default.
htm?referrer=home">
<IMG
src="/NR/fordcom/images/en/global/go.gif"
width="12" height="13"
border="0" alt="Go" align="top"></A></TD>
            </TR>
        </TABLE>
    </DIV>

    <TABLE border="0" cellpadding="0"
cellspacing="0" width="760">
  <TR bgcolor="#CC4400"><TD height="14">
  <IMG
src="/NR/fordcom/images/en/global/nothing.
gif" border="0"
  width="1" height="1" alt=""></TD></TR>
  <TR bgcolor="#CC4400">
    <TD align="center"><IMG src="/NR/
fordcom/images/en/home/welcome.gif"
    border="0" width="585" height="20"
alt="Welcome to ford.com"></TD>
  </TR>
  <TR bgcolor="#CC4400"><TD height="12">
  <IMG
src="/NR/fordcom/images/en/global/nothing.g
if" border="0" width="1"
  height="1" alt=""></TD></TR>
</TABLE>
<TABLE border="0" cellpadding="0"
cellspacing="0" width="760">
<TR>
    <TD valign="top">
    <A
href="/en/heritage/centennial/default.htm?
referrer=home">
    <IMG src="/NR/fordcom/images/en/home/
centennial.jpg" border="0"
    width="174" height="189" alt="100th
Anniversary"></A></TD>
    <TD valign="top"><IMG src="/NR/
fordcom/images/en/home/henry_ford.jpg"
    border="0" width="108" height="189"
alt="Henry Ford"></TD>
    <TD><IMG
src="/NR/fordcom/images/en/global/nothing.
gif" border="0"
    width="40" height="1" alt=""></TD>
    <TD valign="top"><TABLE cellSpacing=0
cellPadding=0 width=165 border=0>
<TBODY>
<TR>
<TD vAlign=top><IMG height=18 alt="For Your
Vehicle"
src="/NR/rdonlyres//for_your_vehicle.gif"
width=165 border=0></TD></TR>
<TR>
<TD class=greyText vAlign=top>
<A href="/NR/Financing.html">Vehicle
Financing</A></TD></TR>
<TR>
...
```

FIGURE 9.2

Ford's website home-page.

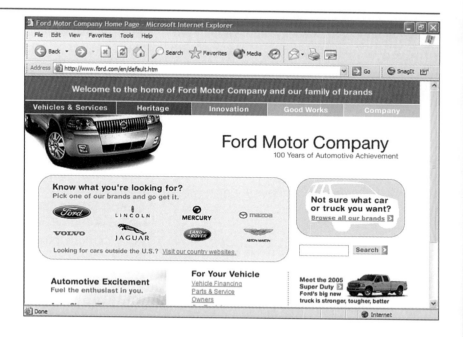

This HTML markup represents only 15% of the entire HTML markup for Ford's homepage! Clearly, having to write the HTML markup for a web page by hand is not an easy task. With tools like Composer, you can specify the formatting and appearance of a web page just like you would with a word processor such as Microsoft Word. When you create or modify a web page with Composer, it automatically generates the HTML for you based on the text, images, and formatting you add to the page.

> **NOTE**
>
> If you are interested in learning the actual markup language of web pages—HTML—consider picking up a copy of *Sams Teach Yourself HTML & XHTML in 24 Hours* (ISBN 0-672-32520-9).

Understanding How the Internet Works

In Chapter 2 you learned of the steps necessary for making the web pages you create accessible to anyone with a connection to the Internet. Recall that you need to host your site with a website host, which will make your website content available on a computer that has a direct and persistent connection to the Internet.

While Chapter 2 covered the steps you need to take to get started publishing your website content, it didn't delve into the specifics of how a web host provider makes your website available to all. Nor did it examine the sequence of steps that happen when a visitor enters your website's URL into their browser. This bonus material explores these areas. With a deeper understanding of how the Internet works, you'll not only better understand *why* you need a web host provider to create a publicly accessible website, but you'll also be able to impress all of your friends and family with your knowledge on this topic!

The secret to understanding how the Internet functions is to realize that the Internet is a lot like the U.S. Postal Service. In the next two sections you'll see how the postal service works and how the Internet's functionality mirrors that of the postal service.

Examining How the Postal Service Works

The U.S. Postal Service allows individuals to send a piece of mail to any address in the world. In order to send a piece of mail, you must do two things:

1. Specify the address to which the mail is to be sent.

2. Drop off the mail at a post office or in a mailbox.

Imagine that you want to send a postcard from your vacation in San Diego, California back to your friend in Albany, New York. You'd first need to write the address of your friend on the postcard: Let's say it's 123 Elm Street, Albany, NY. Then, you drop the postcard in a mailbox.

Sometime later that day, a postal employee will drop by the mailbox, pick up the postcard, and take it back to the post office. Your postcard will get sorted with other incoming mail, and will be placed in a box with other mail that's addressed to residents east of California.

The next day a mail truck will take the letter from the San Diego post office up north to the Los Angeles post office. There, the letter might travel by plane to the post office in New York City, New York. From there, a postal truck will take the postcard up to the Albany post office. Finally, a postal employee in the Albany post office will deliver the mail to your friend's home.

As shown in Figure 9.3, the delivery of mail from San Diego to Albany travels through a number of post offices. What is important to realize is that oftentimes a letter passes through many post offices before reaching its final recipient.

In summary, the U.S. Postal Service has post offices all around the world. A piece of mail is delivered by the sender dropping off an addressed piece of mail to one of these post offices. The piece of mail is then routed through various post offices and finally is delivered directly to the addressed recipient.

The Internet As a Virtual Postal Service

The Internet is setup in a similar fashion to the U.S. Postal Service. The post office can only deliver mail to locations that have a unique address. For postal mail, the address is usually a combination of country, zip code, state or province, street address, and possibly an apartment or suite number. Computers on the Internet are uniquely identified by an *IP address*.

FIGURE 9.3

Mail travels through many post offices on its way to Albany.

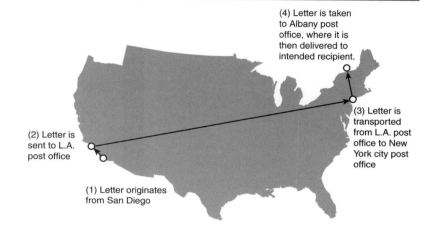

(4) Letter is taken to Albany post office, where it is then delivered to intended recipient.

(3) Letter is transported from L.A. post office to New York city post office

(2) Letter is sent to L.A. post office

(1) Letter originates from San Diego

> **NOTE**
>
> An *IP address* is a series of four numbers, where each number is between 0 and 255. An example of an IP address is 45.102.3.211. The *IP* in IP address stands for Internet Protocol, which, among other things, specifies how computers are addressed on the Internet.

Recall that the postal service has post offices established around the globe to route mail across this planet as needed. The Internet analogy to post offices is *routers*. Routers are specialized computers that do nothing but route Internet traffic from an initial sender to a final receiver. In traversing the Internet, data might travel through upward of 20 routers before reaching its final destination.

Figure 9.4 depicts the path a web page might take when being sent from a web server in San Diego with IP address 134.56.100.76 to your personal computer in Washington D.C. with IP

address 87.213.20.119. Note the similarities between Figures 9.3 and 9.4.

What About Domain Names?

In Chapter 1, "Creating Your First Web Page," we discussed that a website is uniquely identified by a *domain name*, which looks something like www.someName.com, or www.someOtherName.org. However, just a few paragraphs ago I said that computers on the Internet are addressed by an IP address, which has the form XXX.XXX.XXX.XXX, where XXX is a number between 0 and 255. You might rightfully be wondering what relationship there is between domain names and IP addresses.

Recall from Chapter 1 that a website is a collection of web pages that are hosted on a *web server*. A web server is an Internet-connected computer that does nothing other than wait to serve up web pages to requesting web browsers. Since the web server is connected to the Internet, it must be uniquely identified by some IP address.

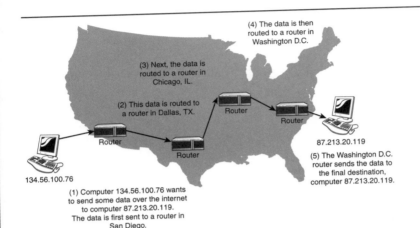

FIGURE 9.4

Internet traffic travels through routers in its trip from sender to receiver.

In fact, you can visit a website by typing its web server's IP address into your browser's Address bar. For example, I can visit the website of my Alma matter—the University of Missouri–Rolla—by either typing in the domain name—www.umr.edu—or its associated IP address—131.151.35.19. Figures 9.5 and 9.6 illustrate that using either the domain name or the IP address takes me to the same website.

FIGURE 9.5

The UMR website, visited by entering its domain name.

FIGURE 9.6

Visiting the UMR website by IP address.

Now, imagine that the only way to access a website was by entering in its IP address. Do you think you could remember the IP address for more than just one or two websites? If you called your parents on the phone and wanted to tell them about the new family website you and your wife were starting, do you think your parents would remember the website IP address if you said, "Just visit 64.123.99.7."?

The IP addressing system was designed with computers in mind. Computers work very well with numbers. Humans, however, remember words and phrases much better. Therefore, to make website addresses more memorable, a *domain name system* was established.

Figure 9.7 shows the sequence of steps your web browser actually goes through when you type the domain name of a website into the Address bar.

Armed with a better understanding of how the Internet works, hopefully it is becoming more clear as to what steps are needed to create a public website, and why. In order to have others be able to view your web pages from their computers, you need to copy your web pages to a computer that has a persistent connection to the Internet. This is done by finding a *web host provider*, a company that offers such services. Next, you'll probably want to create a domain name for the site, which, as we saw in Chapter 2, can be accomplished by leasing a domain name with any domain name registrar, such as Network Solutions. When registering the domain name you'll need to configure the domain name to point to your web server. Finally, you'll need to upload your web pages from your computer to the web server.

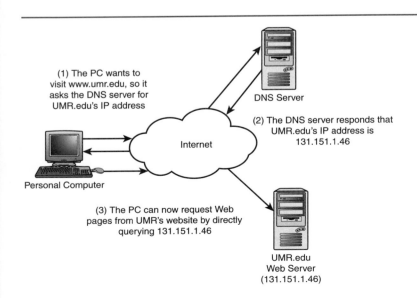

FIGURE 9.7

A DNS server is consulted to discover the IP address for a given domain name.

(1) The PC wants to visit www.umr.edu, so it asks the DNS server for UMR.edu's IP address

DNS Server

(2) The DNS server responds that UMR.edu's IP address is 131.151.1.46

Internet

Personal Computer

(3) The PC can now request Web pages from UMR's website by directly querying 131.151.1.46

UMR.edu
Web Server
(131.151.1.46)

This concludes the examination of how the Internet works. The next section examines how to optimize the digital pictures you place on your website.

Optimizing Your Digital Pictures

In Chapter 3, "Creating a Family/Personal Website," you learned how to customize the website templates by adding your own digital images. With today's technology, adding a digital image is as simple as taking a picture with a digital camera, or scanning a printed image with a scanner. In either case, the resulting digital image may not be ideal—it may be too wide or too tall, or it might be a very large file, which will increase the amount of time it takes for your visitors to load up one of your web pages. Fortunately, optimizing your digital images is relatively straightforward, as you'll see in this section.

When talking about digital images there are a couple of units of measurement that are essential to understand:

▶ The image's file size

▶ The image's width and height

Like any file in a computer, a digital image has a *file size*. The file size specifies how much space the image takes up on the computer's hard drive.

In addition to its file size, a digital image has a certain width and height. For digital images, the width and height is measured in a unit called *pixels* rather than in inches or centimeters. There is no direct translation from pixels

to inches, or vice versa. This is because a given image's height and width in inches varies on the computer monitor being used to view the image. That is, even though an image might be 200 pixels wide by 150 pixels high, one person's computer monitor might show the image as 3 inches by 2 inches, while another's might show the same image as 3.5 inches by 2.75 inches.

> *"Since the computer's physical dimensions and resolution can differ from monitor to monitor, there's no universal translation from pixels to inches or the other way around."*

This discrepancy is due to a number of factors. First, monitors vary in height and width from one another. For example, my laptop screen is 15" wide and 14" high, while my desktop computer's monitor is 17" wide by 17" high. Furthermore, monitors can run at different *resolutions*.

NOTE

A computer monitor's *resolution* indicates how many pixels are displayed horizontally and vertically. Common resolutions are 640×400, 800×600, 1024×768, 1280×1024, and 1600×1200.

Since the computer's physical dimensions and resolution can differ from monitor to monitor, there's no universal translation from pixels to inches or the other way around.

When displaying digital images online, both the image's file size and height and width can impact the user's viewing experience. Digital images with a large file size can take an extraordinarily long time to download, especially over slower dial-up connections to the Internet. Therefore, if your website has numerous large digital images shown on a particular page, it may take tens of seconds, if not minutes, for users to be able to view all of the pictures.

The image's height and width is important too. If the image is larger than 640 pixels wide by 400 pixels high, for users whose monitors are at the 640×400 resolution, the image will be larger than the browser window, meaning they'll have to scroll vertically or horizontally to view all parts of the image. Also, if you are displaying many images in a page in a storyboard-like format, exceptionally wide or tall images can make the web page look crowded and hard to read and enjoy.

> **TIP**
>
> An image's file size and width and height are correlated. That is, images with a smaller width and height typically have a smaller file size. Therefore, by making your images less wide and tall, you'll be making the file's image size less too, which will decrease the amount of time it takes your visitors to download your images.

Resizing Digital Images

Depending on the quality of digital camera you own, the digital images saved by the camera might be quite large in both their height and width and their file size. More often than not, you'll want to resize these images so that they're smaller both in file size and in their dimensions.

There are a number of software tools that can be used to resize a digital image. If you own a digital camera, chances are it came with such a program. If you do not own a digital camera, or if your camera did not come with such software, you can either download the appropriate software or use online tools to resize images.

> **TIP**
>
> A good, free software program for resizing digital images is IrFanView, which is available for download at its website, http://www.irfanview.com/.
>
> There are also websites online that will resize images for you. For example, at http://eee.uci.edu/toolbox/imageresize/ there's an image resize tool. The resizing occurs by selecting an image from your computer, which is then uploaded to their web server and automatically resized. You are then shown the resized image in your browser, and can save it back to your computer's hard drive.

Let's take a look at resizing an image using the image resize tool at http://eee.uci.edu/toolbox/imageresize/. Figure 9.8 shows a digital image I took of my dog Sam. The digital camera saves the photo at a rather high resolution—1152 pixels wide and 864 pixels high. Also the image clocks in at over 360 *kilobytes*.

A *kilobyte*, often abbreviated *KB*, is a common unit of measurement for computer files—one kilobyte is approximately 1,000 bytes. To put things into perspective, dial-up users can optimally download about 56 kilo*bits* per second. There are 8 bits per byte, so a 56 kbps modem can download around 7 kilobytes per second. Therefore, a 360KB file would take over 50 seconds to download on a dial-up connection! This is why it's important to resize your large digital images.

Let's look at how to resize this image to a more acceptable height and width. Start by visiting http://eee.uci.edu/toolbox/imageresize/ in your browser. This web page, shown in Figure 9.9, prompts you to select an image to upload for resizing.

Click the Browse button to select a file from your computer's hard drive. Once you have chosen the file to resize, click the Upload Image button.

FIGURE 9.8
A picture of Sam (taken with a digital camera).

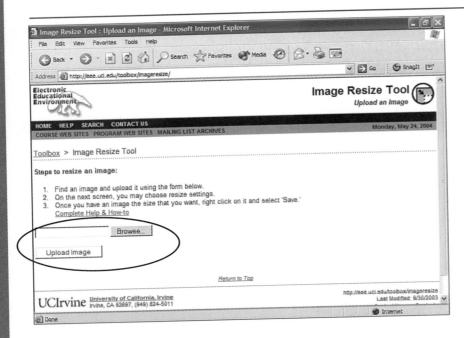

FIGURE 9.9
The Image Resize Tool
helps you resize your
digital images.

NOTE

Clicking the Upload Image button will cause the image to be uploaded from your computer to the web server. If you are connecting over a dial-up connection this could take upward of 50 seconds! Therefore, resizing large images online is only an option for those who have a broadband connection or much patience. If you have a dial-up connection, consider downloading IrFanView for resizing images.

Once you have uploaded the image, you will be taken to a page that displays the uploaded image, its dimensions, and its file size. You are then prompted to select how to resize the image. You can reduce its size either by a specified percentage, or by entering in an absolute width and height in pixels. I am going to opt to resize the picture of Sam down to 320 pixels wide. After typing 320 into the Width textbox the Height textbox automatically is filled in with the value 240. This is the recommended height in pixels to maintain the image's *aspect ratio*.

NEW TERM

The *aspect ratio* is the ratio of the width to the height of the image. When resizing images it is wise to maintain the aspect ratio. If you don't, the image will look squished, as its resized width and height will not be proportional to its original width and height.

Figure 9.10 contains a screenshot of the browser after entering the desired resize width of 320 pixels.

The last step is to click the Resize button. Doing so will display the resized image alongside the original, as shown in Figure 9.11. Note that the resized image's file size is a mere 11.8KB compared to the original's 360KB! This resized image will only take a dial-up user two seconds to download, as compared to 50 or more for the original.

The last step is to save the resized image. To do this, either click on the Save this Image button or right-click on the resized image and choose Save Picture As. In either case, you will be prompted for the file's name and location.

When you plan on displaying digital images from your digital camera or scanner on your website, be sure to take a few minutes to first optimize these images. It will make your site look better to have properly sized images, and will improve your visitor's experience by decreasing the time it takes for them to fully download your web pages.

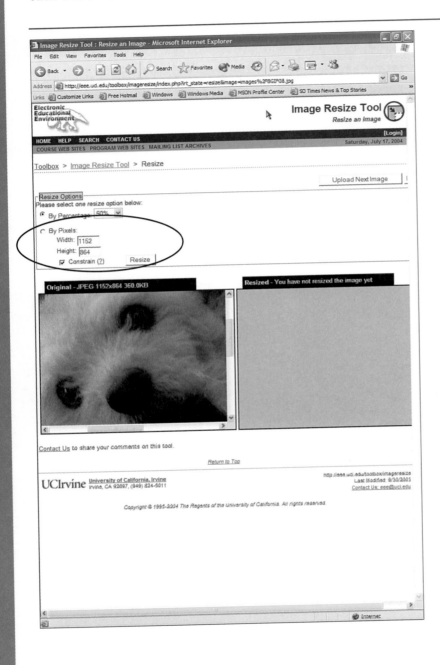

FIGURE 9.10

The image will be
resized to 320×240.

FIGURE 9.11
The resized image is
shown alongside the
original.

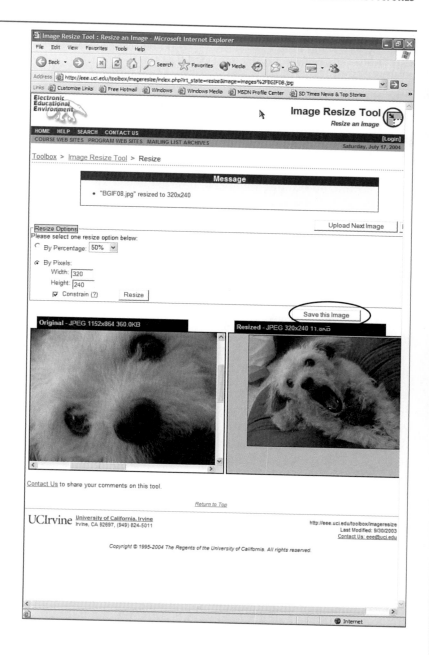

Summary

This chapter presented a number of periphery topics. It provided in-depth information on the fundamental underpinnings of both web pages and the Internet.

In this chapter, you learned that web pages are, in fact, composed of a markup language called *HTML*—while editors like Composer make creating and editing web pages a breeze, under the covers they are really creating and editing HTML documents. You also learned about how the Internet works, how each computer on the Internet is assigned an *IP address*, and how *routers* on the Internet direct traffic much like post offices do with mail. Additionally, the Internet contains a number of *DNS servers*, which provide a mapping from *domain names* to IP addresses. These DNS servers allow you to associate a domain name, like www.msn.com, with an IP address.

The chapter also examined various techniques for optimizing your digital images. If you plan on displaying digital images you took with a digital camera, or ones that you created by using a scanner, it behooves you to first optimize these images to ensure that they have ideal dimensions and file size. By optimizing your images you ensure your visitors will have a more enjoyable experience at your website.

Index

What's on the CD-ROM

The companion CD-ROM contains the Mozilla Suite and the templates developed for the book.

Windows Installation Instructions

1. Insert the disc into your CD-ROM drive.

2. From the Windows desktop, double-click the My Computer icon.

3. Double-click the icon representing your CD-ROM drive.

4. Double-click the icon titled start.exe to run the installation program.

5. Follow the on-screen prompts to finish the installation.

NOTE

If you have the AutoPlay feature enabled, the START.EXE program starts automatically whenever you insert the disc into your CD-ROM drive.

Mac OS X Installation Instructions

1. Insert the disc into your CD-ROM drive.

2. From the Mac desktop, double-click the icon representing your CD-ROM drive.

3. Double-click the icon titled Start to run the installation program.

4. Follow the onscreen prompts to finish the installation.